For Karen

A NEW APPROACH TO
INDONESIAN
COOKING

Selamat makan dan

selamat memasak

Bali, January 14 2015

A NEW APPROACH TO
INDONESIAN COOKING

HEINZ VON HOLZEN

Marshall Cavendish
Cuisine

DEDICATION

To my wife Puji for her love and never ending support. I often ask myself why I deserve such an incredible, kind and loving person by my side.

To Bali, her great people have definitely made me a much better person. Thank you so much for allowing me to be part of your incredible heritage.

To my teams, who never fail to support me wholeheartedly in whatever challenging ideas and ventures I may embark on.

To my most valuable guests and friends, who make my everyday existence possible. You guys lay the foundation for my culinary adventures.

Editor: Melissa Tham
Designer: Lynn Chin
Photographer: Heinz von Holzen

Published by Marshall Cavendish Cuisine
An imprint of Marshall Cavendish International

Other Marshall Cavendish Offices:
Marshall Cavendish Corporation. 99 White Plains Road, Tarrytown NY 10591-9001, USA • Marshall
Cavendish International (Thailand) Co Ltd. 253 Asoke, 12th Flr, Sukhumvit 21 Road, Klongtoey Nua,
Wattana, Bangkok 10110, Thailand • Marshall Cavendish (Malaysia) Sdn Bhd, Times Subang, Lot 46,
Subang Hi-Tech Industrial Park, Batu Tiga, 40000 Shah Alam, Selangor Darul Ehsan, Malaysia

Marshall Cavendish is a trademark of Times Publishing Limited

National Library Board, Singapore Cataloguing-in-Publication Data
Holzen, Heinz von, author.
A new approach to Indonesian cooking / Heinz von Holzen.
– Singapore : Marshall Cavendish Cuisine, 2014. pages cm
ISBN : 978-981-4408-41-7 (paperback)

1. Cooking, Indonesian.   2. Formulas, recipes, etc. – Indonesia   I. Title

TX724.5.I5
641.59598 -- dc23   OCN887101282

Printed by Times Offset Malaysia Sdn Bhd

CONTENTS

RECITES

ACKNOWLEDGEMENTS

I thank my wife Puji for her patience and never ending support. It takes a lot to keep up with my pace and my continuous drive for new and often rather eccentric ideas, especially since a great many hills and mountains needed to be conquered in preparation for this book.

Travelling is one thing but then I needed to get all these great new toys, like blenders, mincers, vacuum packers, pressure cookers and a blowtorch, then another slow cooker and by now we have accumulated thermometers in every corner of our home. Well someone had to pay for all this "absolutely" essential gadgets, and Puji willingly paid for all this equipments which look great in our kitchen now. Unfortunately we have no more space on our shelves and I am already thinking of building another kitchen….Puji you are terrific.

Next, a very big thank you to my best Bali friend for the past 22 years who is also our Development Chef Ida Bagus Wisnawa. He single-handedly prepared each and every dish in this book, (ok there was his kitchen team of mostly ladies assisting him). Well, only God knows how many dishes we prepared and re-photographed several times before the shots were ready for the book. I am not quite certain how Pak Bagus manages to keep up with my pace…I guess the fact that we both learned so many new techniques and skills which we not only feature in this publication but also implemented in our restaurants, and this book kept us going day after day. Pak Bagus you are a champion.

My deepest gratitude goes to several people whom I have never met but still admire from the bottom of my heart. Culinary geniuses and champions of our trade. Harold McGee for his publication *On Food and Cooking: The Science and Lore of the Kitchen*. A scientist who dramatically changed my way of thinking about food. Thank you Heston Blumenthal, a most extraordinary Chef who has done so much incredible work and research and published several world class publications. Then there is *The Modernist Cuisine*, which simply has to be the greatest cookbook ever produced. What an incredible source of information that guided me throughout the preparation of this book. Lastly, I should not forget *Pauli*, the cookbook used in my culinary school in Switzerland. This book has been with me since 1975 when I embarked on my culinary journey around the globe. A publication which is now available as an application for your computer. Thank you all so much and please keep up your terrific work.

A very special thank you to my very good friend from Ternate in the Spice Islands, Miss Meidy Parengkuana, for organising the five private cooks from the Sultan of Ternate and preparing the Sultan's favourite ceremonial dishes for me.

Next we fly across Indonesia to Sumatra, where Pak Dian Anugrah opened my eyes to Padang cuisine and then later travelled for two weeks to Bali, helping us to prepare for all the delicate recipes in this book from Sumatra. He revealed to me the secret to preparing a traditional Sumatran *rendang*.

During a week-long visit to Makassar in South Sulawesi, I met Faisal Akbar Zaenal, his gracious mom and Mr. Aldyno. The two young men were expert cooks who brought me to every interesting eatery in town and introduced me to the delicious flavours of their island. During the photoshoot for this book, these two great gentlemen flew to Bali and helped with the preparation of their local specialties. This also gave us the certainty that each and every dish and recipe would be as authentic as the ones on the streets of Makassar.

Many of the dishes presented are produced by Jenggala Keramik's fabulous table and china ware. I am most grateful that I was able to borrow many pieces from their private collection.

Finally to the world's greatest teams in Bumbu Bali, Restaurant & Cooking School and Rumah Bali Bed & Breakfast. They all stood behind me every minute of every day in a way that only friends would. There is absolutely nothing I would be able to achieve without their wholehearted commitment towards my great many cultural and culinary activities. You will be in my heart forever.

INTRODUCTION

When I was approached by Marshall Cavendish to write another cookbook on Indonesian cuisine, I agreed without a second thought. To ensure the accuracy of the recipes and that instructions for reproducing the original flavour of each dish are clear, chefs from various parts of Indonesia were flown in to help with the preparation of their respective regional specialities. As we progressed, however, my chefs and I decided to venture in a slightly different direction, given the enthusiastic response of the participants in the cooking classes we conducted. Three times a week, we take 14 guests to the local market, where we look at the relationship between people, food and culture in Bali. We purchase the ingredients for the day's class and prepare dishes with the participants. During class, we examine Balinese cuisine from every possible angle. Apart from teaching traditional ways of preparing dishes, we also introduce them to the latest cooking techniques.

Influenced by Harold McGee (American food scientist), Heston Blumenthal (chef extraordinaire from the UK), Nathan Myhrvold and Maxime Bilet (authors of *Modernist Cuisine*) and Philip Pauli (author of the incredibly inspiring *Classical Cooking: The Modern Way*), my chefs and I began to do things differently. We started to brine meats, cook fish in a vacuum and make use of slow cookers and pressure cookers. We paid attention to the science of cooking and this led to incredible improvements to almost every dish. Participants in our cooking classes loved this approach and they inspired us to search for new ways to improve cooking methods. I came to the realisation that the latest cooking techniques actually have a place in Indonesian traditional cuisine just as they do in modern Western cuisine.

After months of research and testing, I am proud to present this collection of Indonesian recipes prepared using new techniques. Although the cooking methods do veer from the usual, the selection of dishes showcases the variety and authentic taste of Indonesian cuisine. It is my hope that you will be inspired by these cooking techniques and incorporate them in your daily cooking.

Heinz von Holzen

THE CUISINE OF INDONESIA

The Indonesian archipelago is made up of over 17,000 islands, and about one-third is inhabited.

Understandably, the cuisine is diverse across the regions. Adding to the diversity are the foreign influences brought about by international trading. Throughout its history, Indonesia has had traders bringing in produce from India, the Middle East, China and Europe, all of whom have had great influences on indigenous cuisine.

Dishes from Sumatra, for example, often include meat and vegetable curries, an influence from Middle Eastern and Indian cuisine. Chinese or Southeast Asian elements are also apparent in some Indonesian food such as *bakmi* (meatball noodles), *mie ayam* (chicken noodle) with *pangsit* (wonton), *mie goreng* (fried noodles), *kwetiau goreng* (fried flat rice noodles), *bakso* (meat or fish balls) and *lumpia* (spring rolls).

And similarly, Indonesian food has also had an impact on other cuisines. *Tempeh*, a fermented soybean cake that originated in Java, is now popular across Asia, particularly in Southeast Asia. *Rendang sapi* (beef braised in coconut milk), *tahu* (tofu) and various types of *sambals* (spiced sauces) with Indonesian roots are now also popular outside the archipelago.

To gather recipes for this book, I travelled to parts of Indonesia that I had not previously visited, or rarely visited. I flew to the Maluku Islands in search of spices like nutmeg, cloves, cinnamon and pepper. I went to Padang to learn how to make one of Indonesia's imperial dishes, the renowned beef *rendang*. I went across Sumatra to Palembang, savouring classic favourites such as *pempek* (fish cake) and *tek wan* (fish ball soup).

As such, you will find that the recipes in this book contain many gems rarely featured in other English cookbooks, including dishes that originate from Flores, Sulawesi and other less travelled regions. From the extensive research and travels I have conducted for this book, I have come to realise that Indonesian food uses a wide array of spices for flavour. Very often, it is the condiment that make Indonesian food spicy. These condiments are served separately with every meal, and I have included a section in this book dedicated to these great little dishes that contribute so much to the taste and flavour of Indonesian cuisine.

It has been an incredible journey, during which I met many amazing people. Indeed, Indonesia is a magnificent country, home not only to a rich and diverse cuisine, but also to some of the kindest and most hospitable people I know.

COOKING EQUIPMENT & UTENSILS

No specialised equipment is necessary in traditional Indonesian cooking. Most dishes can be prepared using widely available tools found in Western kitchens.

I would, however, recommend using good quality cooking utensils, particularly pots and pans, so that optimum heat control can be achieved during cooking.

MORTAR AND PESTLE

The mortar and pestle are important tools for grinding and crushing ingredients, in particular for making spice pastes, which are key to the flavours of Indonesian cuisine. Choose a mortar that is slightly curved, heavy, sturdy and roughly textured, preferably carved from volcanic rock. A rough stone mortar is best for grinding ingredients by hand.

FOOD PROCESSOR, BLENDER AND MEAT GRINDER

These tools are common even in Indonesian kitchens. They are modern conveniences that are especially popular when preparing food for large groups of people. Many spice mixtures can be ground or chopped using a food processor or blender, and a meat grinder is useful for mincing meat or seafood in big quantities. When using a food processor, ingredients should first be roughly chopped before processing with a little oil and water. Use a blender if a smoother texture is required.

POTS AND PANS

High quality stainless-steel or copper pans are a good investment for any kitchen. These items can withstand long-term use and resist the corrosive action of food ingredients and cleaning compounds. Good pots and pans do not transfer unwanted odours, colours or flavours to the food during cooking. Good pans also distribute heat much more evenly, preventing hot spots that can cause burning and sticking.

STEAMER

A steamer comes with a perforated insert that fits nicely in a pan, as well as a snug-fitting lid to cover the food while steaming. Simple stainless-steel steamer inserts are widely available and can often fit in pots and pans of different sizes. Use a heavy glass cover so that you can monitor the cooking process without lifting the lid.

WOK

Contrary to Western belief, woks are seldom used in the preparation of foods in Indonesia. However, when using a wok, a heavy steel version with a diameter of 30-35 cm is best.

RICE COOKER

Indonesians eat a substantial amount of rice and, very often, a large group will eat together. A rice cooker is therefore essential in their homes. A heavy saucepan with a perforated insert and a heavy tight lid can also be used to cook rice. Once the rice is done, the rice cooker switches to a "keep warm" mode, so there is no need to keep watch while the rice is cooking.

Regardless of whether the rice is cooked using traditional or modern equipment, soaking the washed rice grains in fresh water for about 25 minutes before cooking is essential to ensure that the rice will not overcook or stick to the bottom of the pot.

1. Hand Blender   2. Rice Cooker   3. Measuring Cups   4. Stone Mortar   5. Steamer   6. Slow Cooker   7. Sous Vide Machine   8. Wok
9. Thermometer   10. Sausage Stuffer   11. Vacuum Packing Machine

SLOW COOKER

One of the biggest enemies in the kitchen is high heat. Invest in a good quality slow cooker so that temperatures can be digitally controlled. This useful gadget allows you to start a stew in the morning that will continue cooking even while you are at the office. After returning from a hard day's work, all you will need to do is season the stew and it will be ready for serving. See the section on sous vide on page 34 for instructions on how to prepare delicious meals in a slow cooker. Follow the same steps but instead of packing food in a plastic bag, place it straight into the slow cooker and set the same temperature as you would for sous vide.

WATER BATH

This is essentially cooking food in a plastic bag submerged in water. In order to perfectly cook a dish, it requires bringing it to a specific core temperature. To achieve this, the chef requires a medium that can control cooking temperatures to the degree. This can be done with a heatproof plastic bag and a digitally-controlled water bath. If you do not wish to invest in such an equipment, all you need is a heavy pot large enough to hold 5–7 litres of water and an accurate thermometer. Seal the food in a heatproof plastic bag and remove the air, preferably via a vacuum packing machine, and then place inside the water bath and set the desired temperature. This simple technique allows the chef to cook food evenly at the exact temperature desired without any danger of overcooking.

DIGITAL THERMOMETER

Small changes in temperature can make all the difference in cooking, and a digital thermometer is necessary for ensuring that each dish is cooked at the correct temperature. Many recipes in this book provide the optimum temperature for cooking a dish and using a digital thermometer will enable you to follow the recipes closely, thus yielding the best results.

HAND BLENDER

The hand blender is a very useful tool for aerating soups and sauces and blending sauces and *sambals* in small quantities. It is also terrific for foaming up sauces, especially for dishes containing coconut cream. A professional hand blender with durable motors is best.

VACUUM PACKING MACHINE

This machine is useful when cooking sous vide. The reasons for packaging food without air before placing in a water bath are simple: most unpacked foods get messy in a water bath, while air-filled bags float, resulting in unevenly cooked food. Air is also a poor heat conductor, so the food will heat faster and more uniformly without air around it. More importantly, water evaporates from the food into the air, causing the food to cool and dry out; but if air is removed from the bag, moisture will be locked in. Food operators that cook sous vide vacuum-seal the food in special plastic bags that are less likely to float. This also enables cooked food to keep longer in the refrigerator, which is handy for commercial operations that prepare large quantities of food in advance. Vacuum packing machines for home use are now widely available and easy to use.

KNIVES

Both Western and Indonesian cooks use a variety of knives. Because many meats, fish and spices require chopping, a heavy chopping knife should always be at hand. Various smaller knives are also needed to clean, cut, trim and slice vegetables, fruits, meats or spices. Knives made from stainless steel are best, as they are affordable and resistant to corrosion.

CHOPPING BOARDS

Meats and fish used in Indonesian cooking can often be tough or very dry, so they need to be chopped or pounded into a mince. Therefore, a heavy chopping board is very useful. For safety and sanitation, do not use one chopping board for all tasks. Instead, use several boards of different colours for fish, meat, vegetables and fruits to prevent cross contamination of food.

GRATER AND SHREDDER

High quality stainless-steel graters and shredders are useful for grating vegetables, coconuts, nutmegs or limes. They are also great for zesting limes.

DIGITAL SCALE

A digital scale takes out all the guesswork in cooking and a good set will provide precise measurements to the gram. Most digital scales can be switched from metric to the US measuring system, making it easy to use. Most recipes in this book require accurate weighing, which will guarantee consistency no matter how many times you cook the dish. It is absolutely essential to follow the given weights for spice mixes and blends as accurately as possible. This will ensure that the spice blends taste authentic.

As all recipes in this book are based on metric measures, we recommend following the stated amounts in the recipes carefully. As such, it is crucial to get an electronic scale with a range from 1 g to 2 kg.

PRESSURE COOKER

Wonderful aromas wafting through the kitchen while you cook may warm your heart and stimulate your appetite, but they are actually some of the most crucial components of the food that are lost from the dish. It should be your aim and biggest challenge to make sure that your kitchen smells of anything but food. This is why the pressure cooker is such a fantastic tool and an absolute must-have for making stocks, sauces, soups, stews and tenderising tough meats.

Where I grew up in my homeland, Switzerland, a pressure cooker was one of the most valuable commodities in my mom's kitchen. To this day, I still remember hearing the screaming and whistling of the pressure cooker as I arrived home from school. I had the impression that a pressure cooker was a housewife's tool and that this noisy cooking equipment from mom's kitchen did not belong in a professional or commercial kitchen. Thirty-five years later, I started experimenting with a small 5-litre pressure cooker and that was when I discovered the real value of this incredibly useful equipment. Today, we use at least 20 of them in our kitchens. From stocks, soups, ribs, ox tongue, mung beans to black rice, almost everything in our kitchens is cooked under pressure.

A pressure cooker is sealed and pressurised during cooking. This has some advantages:

1. Flavours that normally dissipate and fill your kitchen with tantalising aromas will be better retained, resulting in a cooked dish that has a much richer flavour.

2. Liquids can be heated to higher temperatures without vapourising into steam, enabling a greater intensity of flavour to be extracted from the meat and an acceleration of Maillard reactions, producing a more aromatic dish.

3. With higher temperatures and pressures, at least a third of the cooking time is reduced with a pressure cooker.

4. It is great for making clear soups and stocks as it prevents liquid from reaching a boil, which means there is no turbulence to emulsify the oils back into the soup or stock, resulting in a clearer broth. In addition, if the pressure cooker is cooled before opening, the different flavours will condense back into the dish.

The pressure cooker is safe to use, with well-designed pressure limits and a safety valve to prevent ruptures. Simply follow these important points:

1. Read and follow the instruction manual that comes with the pressure cooker.

2. Check that the ring of rubber or silicon lining around the lid is not dry or cracked. These gaskets do not last forever; replace them as recommended by the manufacturer.

3. Always ensure that the inside of the cooker has been de-pressurised before opening the lid. Doing so prematurely can cause hot food and liquid to splatter all over the kitchen or onto you. Follow the manufacturer's instructions for releasing the lid.

4. When preparing food for pressure-cooking, first heat up the food until it boils, and then skim off any scum. Cover and seal the cooker. Once the lid is secure, reduce heat to the minimum and pressure cook at 1 bar or 15 psi. For the older type of jiggle-top pressure cooker, this will mean the valve only releases very small amounts of steam.

5. Do not fill the cooker more than two-thirds full. Food expands when cooked, and over-filling the pressure cooker with food will cause pressure to build up faster, causing safety valves to activate and release pressure, thus affecting how the food is cooked.

6. Most pressure cookers are designed to hold the pressure of water heated to 120°C. If the temperature increases beyond this, then the pressure cooker is designed to release the excess pressure and steam through a vent. When this happens, the water inside the pressure cooker will come to a boil and the stock will end up cloudy, while some of the volatile flavours and aromas will be lost with the escaping steam. It is therefore best to first bring the stew or braise to a boil uncovered, and then reduce the heat and seal the cooker to continue cooking at a pressure of about 15 psi.

Although a pressure cooker does require a little attention and extra care, once you are familiar with its use, it will become your greatest kitchen companion as it yields fantastic results.

Pork in Sweet Soy Sauce (*Be Celeng Base Manis*)

5 Tbsp coconut oil

90 g shallots, peeled
and sliced

60 g garlic, peeled and sliced

1.2 kg boneless pork
shoulder or neck, cut
into 2.5-cm cubes brined
for 5 hours

70 g ginger, peeled, sliced
and bruised

6 Tbsp sweet soy sauce
(*kecap manis*)

3 Tbsp salty soy sauce
(*kecap asin*)

1 pinch black peppercorns,
crushed

600 ml chicken stock
(page 44)

6-10 bird's eye chillies

2-3 large red chillies, whole

cracked black pepper,
to taste

1. Heat coconut oil in a heavy saucepan (pressure cooker pan). Add shallots and garlic and sauté for 2 minutes over medium heat or until lightly coloured. Add pork and ginger. Continue to sauté for 2 more minutes over medium heat. Add sweet and salty soy sauces and crushed black pepper. Continue to sauté for 1 more minute.

2. Pour chicken stock into pan. Add chillies and bring to a simmer. Skim off scum.

3. Pressure cook at a gauge pressure of 1 bar / 15 psi for 25 minutes. Start timing when full pressure is reached. Let the cooker cool for 20 minutes.

4. Lift the meat from the cooking liquid with a slotted spoon, and transfer to a frying pan.

5. Strain the liquid into a pot. Bring to a simmer and skim off as much fat as possible.

6. Transfer 250 ml (1 cup) of the cooking liquid to the saucepan and simmer over medium heat, gently turning and basting the meat for 12-15 minutes until it is glazed. Reduce the remaining liquid by half and add to the meat. Mix well and simmer for 2 more minutes over low heat.

7. Remove from heat, and let the mixture infuse for 7–10 minutes.

8. Season to taste with black pepper.

COOKING TECHNIQUES

Traditional Indonesian cooking techniques are very simple. In the past, the main source of heat was a simple wood fire.

Today, kerosene or gas stoves are used. Cooking vessels are mostly made from sheet iron or aluminium; occasionally a wok is used. Indonesians mostly use very low heat to cook their dishes, so it is important to set aside plenty of time when preparing food. The key is in the mixing and blending of spices. Therefore, it is both important and rewarding to use only the freshest ingredients that are easily available in most Asian markets and stores.

BLANCHING

Blanching is a simple cooking technique that is great for preparing vegetables. Follow the ratio of 10 parts water to 1 part vegetables. Water is first brought to a rapid boil before adding the vegetables. When the water returns to a boil, remove and drain vegetables and plunge immediately into cold water to stop the cooking process. For delicate vegetables such as green beans, a quick blanch is sufficient to ensure that they stay crisp. Larger vegetables require a longer cooking time in order to soften their fibres while still retaining just enough firmness for a crunchy bite.

It is best to blanch food in batches, especially when cooking a larger quantity as this helps to ensure the water remains at boiling temperature. This also applies when cooking in other liquids such as sauces or stocks. Imagine dipping a hand into a tub of hot water. It would feel even hotter when you run your hand through it rather than keeping still, because the flowing water would not have time to cool against your skin by transferring heat to your hand, making it feel hotter. Based on the same principle, the rapid movement of boiling water heats up the food more quickly than water that has not boiled, which is why it is important to keep water at a rolling boil when blanching food. An overcrowded pot can also make the water temperature drop, causing food to cook more slowly, leading to the loss of flavour, colour and nutrients.

Blanching can also cleanse bones meant for stocks. To do so, place thoroughly washed bones into cold water before bringing slowly to a boil. This will open up the pores of the bones and clean out the impurities. Discard the water and use the bones for preparing stock.

Blanching

Boiling and Simmering

Poaching

BOILING AND SIMMERING

Unlike boiling, where food is cooked in rapidly moving liquid, simmering is a cooking process where food is cooked in liquid that is just below boiling point. Simmering liquid has very light, trembling movements, with small bubbles forming. When boiling or simmering food, it is important to first establish if the food should be placed into cold or hot liquid. Note the following:

1. Always add rice or noodles into rapidly boiling liquid to prevent sticking. Stir frequently. Do not cover when cooking starchy food such as rice and noodles, as this will cause the temperature to rise and result in overcooking.

2. Follow the ratio of 10 parts liquid to 1 part pasta or noodles.

3. Meats such as chicken or beef should be added into simmering liquid or stock. Do not cover, as this will intensify the heat, causing the stock to turn cloudy.

4. For mung beans and black rice, start with cold liquid, bring to a fast boil, reduce heat and then simmer over a low flame until done. Do not cover.

5. As with blanching, boil food in batches to maintain a rolling boil.

POACHING

Poaching is a gentler cooking process than blanching, boiling or simmering. It involves cooking food below boiling point to retain its beneficial properties such as vitamins and minerals. The food to be poached is added to liquid heated to 50–80°C, where it will be cooked until done at a consistent temperature. Poaching can be used for sausages, fish, eggs, dumplings, fruits, sweet snacks, etc. Never cover when poaching food, as this will increase heat, causing the liquid to boil and the food to discharge vitamins and minerals, leading to a loss of flavour, colour, shape and texture. Poaching is perfect for sous vide cooking (page 34).

Steaming

STEAMING

As the name suggests, it is the hot steam that cooks the food in this method. Simple equipment like a pot or wok can function as a steamer. Simply bring water in the steamer to a boil, and then position a rack inside with the food on top of the rack. Cover with a heavy-fitting lid and the cooking process begins.

Both Western and Asian cooking traditions have settled on steaming as the preferred method for cooking certain dishes because it is a gentle cooking process that retains the shape and texture of food. For this reason, whole fishes are commonly steamed so that their delicate flesh remains firm and do not fall apart. In the Western kitchen, cooks commonly steam small pieces of vegetables or thin slices of fish and other seafood. In the Asian kitchen, vegetables are usually stir-fried, and meats, seafood and dumplings are typically steamed.

In Indonesia, steaming is a very popular cooking method that is used almost daily to cook parcels of meat, fish, rice, vegetables, sausages and sweet snacks wrapped in banana leaves. However, in Flores, an island east of Java, traditional steaming techniques are usually reserved for food cooked in bamboo poles.

While steaming and boiling are both healthier compared to other cooking techniques, steaming has one major advantage compared to boiling. Much of the natural sugars, colours and vitamins of food are diluted during boiling, as they dissolve readily in water and are leached out during the boiling process. Carrots, for example, taste more bland when boiled instead of steamed. As steaming cooks food with hot air, the food retains more of the natural sugars and vitamins that give the dish its distinctive flavours and colours. Hence, while steaming may take slightly longer than boiling, it often yields vegetables that look and taste better. It is also easier to steam rather than boil large quantities of food, since there is no need to cook in batches to maintain the rolling boil of water.

Sautéing and Pan-frying

Grilling and Broiling

Deep-Frying

SAUTÉING AND PAN-FRYING

These two cooking techniques are frequently used interchangeably although there are differences between them. Both methods cook food using direct conduction of heat from a hot metal pan. A thin layer of oil is required to coat the pan to prevent sticking. Oil also conducts heat more evenly from the pan to the food.

Sautéing is cooking small pieces of food over high heat until they brown in a matter of seconds. The food is tossed frequently so that it is browned and cooked evenly. Pan-frying refers to cooking larger portions of food over heat that is high enough to sear, but at a lower temperature than when sautéing.

Both techniques require maintaining a high temperature even while moisture from the food is being vapourised. If the pan cools enough to let moisture accumulate – for example, because it was insufficiently heated, or overloaded with cold wet meat – then the food will stew in its own juices and its surface will not brown well. The same thing will happen if the pan is covered, as the condensation from the steam will be trapped and drip back into the pan. The appetizing sizzle of frying meat is actually the sound of moisture from the meat being vapourised as it hits the hot metal pan, and many cooks use this sound to judge the temperature of the pan. A strong continuous hiss indicates the immediate conversion of moisture to steam, leading to efficient surface browning.

GRILLING AND BROILING

Both grilling and broiling involve cooking food over an open flame. The main difference is that for grilling, the heat source is below the food, and for broiling, the heat source is above. Oxygen is needed for fire to burn. As the fire takes in oxygen from the surrounding air, which gets heated and rises as a result, cooler air with more oxygen rushes in as replacement. This creates a draft that brings in oxygen continuously to sustain the flames. Fanning the fire creates a greater draft and therefore makes it burn faster and hotter. A master griller stokes a fire by raking coals around or adjusting a vent under the grill. Rarely will he add more coals. He fans the fire to control the draft – a skill that is acquired with experience. Increase the draft by too much and the fire will grow too hot and burn the food. Reduce the draft drastically and it can cause smouldering, leading to lack of heat, and affecting cooking time and results. To facilitate the control of fire, charcoal is often used. Charcoal has many advantages compared to wood. It burns cleaner, hotter and more evenly than wood. It also lasts longer. However, hot coals cool slowly, so the draft should be adjusted well before you want the temperature to drop.

DEEP-FRYING

This is the most widely used cooking method throughout Indonesia, but it is often not done correctly in the average household, making it an unhealthy and fattening way of cooking. However, if done correctly, deep-frying can prove to be most satisfying.

Fats and oils are a useful cooking medium as they can be heated to temperatures well above the boiling point of water and can dry, crisp and brown the food surface easily. The usual deep-frying temperature is between 120–175°C. For larger pieces that are deep-fried, pre-cooking at a lower temperature is recommended before deep-frying to thoroughly cook and brown them just before serving.

Oil is not only a cooking medium that transfers heat to the food, but it is also an ingredient that is part of the dish. Heat cooks oil as well, and the way that oil changes during heating has a profound impact on whether the food cooked in it will be appealing or appalling.

It is therefore important to choose a suitable type of oil and handle it correctly.

Deep-fried food is usually coated in batter.

Batter for Deep-frying

This is a basic frying batter for coating fish, meat, tofu, tempeh, vegetables or fruits. As a gluten-free alternative, regular wheat flour can be replaced with rice flour, which will result in an even, crispier crust.

$2/3$ cup rice flour, sifted + more for dusting
$1/3$ cup wheat flour, sifted
$2/3$ cup water
a pinch of salt

1. Combine rice flour, wheat flour, water and salt in a deep mixing bowl. Whisk into a smooth batter.

2. Pass the batter through a sieve to remove any lumps. It should be the consistency of pancake batter.

3. Lightly dust ingredients with rice flour before dipping into the batter to coat evenly. Allow excess batter to drip off before lowering into hot oil for deep-frying.

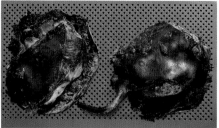

Stir-frying   Roasting   Braising

STIR-FRYING

Stir-frying with a wok is actually a Chinese cooking method that is seldom employed for Indonesian cuisine. Originally a thin shell of iron, a Chinese wok today is commonly forged from carbon steel, a stronger material that can also withstand high heat. Regardless of the wok material, the patina must be present. A patina provides a protective barrier that inhibits rust and prevents food from sticking.

The wok is set over an open flame and heated to very high temperatures for cooking. As with sautéing and pan-frying, water should not accumulate during a stir-fry as that could result in stewing rather than stir-frying the food. High heat is required for moisture to evaporate, and even higher temperatures are needed to achieve the sought-after *wok hei* (pronounced as "hay") that lovers of Cantonese cuisine are so familiar with. *Wok hei* is a Cantonese phrase that literally translates to "breath of the wok". It is that distinct flavour of food that has been aromatically charred by well-controlled searing high temperatures. This is the result of intense Maillard reactions at high heat and the fragrance imparted to the food from a highly-heated wok. Amidst a skilled chef's flourishing act of tossing food in a wok and impressive handling of the flaming utensil, complex scientific processes are occurring.

Simply put, food cooks very quickly via direct contact with the highly-heated wok surface. To prevent the food from burning, the chef would toss it into the air after a brief stir-fry, subjecting it to cooler temperatures above the wok surface, which still cooks the food, but at a slower rate. The stir-frying and tossing is repeated until the food is stir-fried to perfection. It takes a skilled chef to know when to toss the wok in order to achieve the desired *wok hei*. It is also important to exercise caution while employing this cooking technique, for at such high temperatures, food can be flammable, which is dangerous if not handled properly.

Because of the extreme temperatures and potentially dangerous manoeuvres required, home cooks are typically unable to reproduce *wok hei*. Western cooking techniques cannot achieve this unique taste as well since extreme high heat over an open flame is required, which Western-style burners cannot produce.

ROASTING

Roasting essentially employs dry heat from an open flame, an oven or other heat sources to cook food. Spit-roasting, also called "rotisserie", is so closely linked to roasting that it is often thought to be an essential feature, but it is not necessarily so. Spit-roasting is done by impaling the meat on a metal skewer or – the preferred method in Indonesia – on a wooden stick to turn the food over a heat source. Traditional roasting in Indonesia is done over an open fire on a spit or, when food is wrapped in various kinds of leaves, buried in hot charcoal.

In a Western kitchen, a standard oven can be used. If spit-roasting is not possible, the cut is roasted in an oven at medium to very low heat and basted frequently with an oil-based marinade. Today, in many parts of Indonesia, large families continue to use traditional roasting methods for cooking whole animals such as pigs and lambs, especially during festive or celebratory occasions, so that there is enough meat to go around. As even piglets and lambs are too large for most ovens, roasting is the ideal method for cooking whole animals, since it is easy to build a fire large enough to slow roast the meat to perfection.

GLAZING

Glazing meat involves coating the cut with a savoury sauce for added flavour and sheen. Stock is reduced until it becomes a concentrated syrup before adding to the meat. A stock glaze can also be a basting liquid for meat browning in the oven. For glazing, the meat to liquid ratio should be 2:1 respectively at the start. Keep the liquid to a minimum, adding small amounts during the cooking process. This ensures that the final sauce will have the right consistency and that the meat has a nice shiny coating.

BRAISING AND STEWING

Braising is a relatively slow and long process for cooking large cuts of meat in liquid. This cooking technique is used for tougher cuts of meat, since the longer cooking process will break down the tough connective tissues in the meat, rendering fork-tender and succulent results. The liquid for braising is usually a stock. Sometimes, liquor is added too. Depending on the chef's preference, the amount of braising liquid varies, but it is usually just enough to partially cover the meat. Beef, lamb, pork, chicken, vegetables and mushrooms can be braised. The resultant braised sauce becomes an aromatic and flavourful part of the dish.

Stewing is often used interchangeably with braising as they are very similar cooking techniques. The difference is that a stew cooks smaller meat pieces of uniform size. More liquid is added to a stew too, as the meat pieces are usually fully submerged.

BRINE

Brining has been used to preserve food since ancient times. It involves immersing meat in a salt solution, often with other ingredients for flavour. If done correctly, brining will not only enhance flavour, but also produce tender and moist meat. It is possible to achieve similar results by rubbing salt directly onto the meat, but this may result in loss of moisture as dry salt draws water out from the meat.

The proportion of salt added and how it is applied to the meat is important, as salt can cure the meat, which is not what brining is supposed to do. Depending on the thickness of the meat, the brining process can take a few hours to two days. During brining, interactions between the salt and the meat proteins will increase the ability of the muscle cells to hold water. At the same time, as the brine changes the muscle structures and dissolves protein filaments within the meat, flavour from the brining ingredients, such as spices and herbs, can be absorbed, and the meat also becomes more tender.

The brine works from outside in and has the strongest effect on parts of the meat that are likely to be overcooked. Therefore, even if the meat has been soaked briefly, it can make a difference. However, as brining makes the final dish saltier, the saltiness can be countered by adding sweet or sour ingredients such as fruit juices or buttermilk.

The following basic brine recipes can also be used for curing. Weigh the meat and water for curing together, making an allowance for the weight of bones and gristle if necessary. The amount of salt added should be 2-3% of the combined weight of the meat and water. Combine with other ingredients such as spices and herbs if using, and vacuum seal everything to start the brining process.

Basic Meat Brine

1 litre water
40 g salt
15 g sugar

Basic Seafood Brine

1 litre water
40 g salt
25 g palm sugar
3 stalks lemongrass, bruised
5 kaffir lime leaves, bruised

1. Combine all the ingredients in a saucepan and bring to a quick boil.

2. Cool to room temperature. Store in refrigerator until ready to use.

Meat

Chicken

Seafood

SMOKING

Smoking is the process of flavouring, cooking, or preserving food by exposing it to the smoke from burning or smouldering plant materials, most often wood. This is a fantastic way to introduce an extra flavour dimension. Most of us are familiar with smoked salmon, trout, or meats like ham or bacon, but almost anything can be smoked. Like curing, smoking is an ancient cooking method that was originally used to preserve food. The smoke would dry the surface, preventing it from going rancid, while some compounds in the smoke would inhibit the activity of microbes and enzymes that would otherwise quickly spoil the food. Smoking can indeed be very addictive once you discover how simple it really is.

Principle of smoking:

Not much is really needed to add a smooth soft smoky flavour to your dishes. Simply use your small BBQ grill and take a small stainless steel container into which you drill a few holes to allow air flow. Next you place some burning charcoal into the bowel and cover with your favorite wood chips. A good way to ignite your charcoal is with a blowtorch. That way you can create a lot of smoke with relatively low heat in the pan. Once the chips smoke, place your goods on to the grill rack, cover the barbecue with the lid or with foil. If your barbecue has some ventilation holes on the bottom, gently blow in a little air and this will keep the charcoal glowing. You do not require a lot of heavy smoke (as this will make your food taste very bitter), but a soft gentle smoke right from the beginning when the chips start to smoke. If you wish to cook your food at the same time as you smoke it, then insert a probe into the goods to be smoked and cook to the required core temperature (see sous vide page 34)

Smoked Fish (*Ikan Asap*)

1.2 kg mackerel fillets, cleaned and deboned (any other oily fish like salmon or trout works equally well)
75 ml coconut or vegetable oil
wood chips for smoking

BRINE
1 litre water
50 g salt
40 g palm sugar
3 stalks lemongrass, bruised
5 kaffir lime leaves, bruised

SPICE BLEND
60 g shallots, peeled and finely sliced
30 g garlic, peeled and finely chopped
40 g large red chillies, halved, seeded and sliced
3-5 bird's eye chillies, finely sliced
30 g ginger, peeled and finely sliced
1/2 Tbsp crushed coriander seeds
1/4 tsp crushed white peppercorns
30 g palm sugar, finely grated

1. To make the spice blend, combine all ingredients in a stone mortar or food processor and grind into a very fine paste.

2. To prepare the brine, combine all ingredients and bring to a quick boil. Add ground spices and bring to a boil again. Turn off heat and allow spices to infuse for 1 hour at room temperature. Cool and store in the refrigerator.

3. Cover fish fillet in a deep container or plastic bag with brine. Cure for 5 hours, or 12 hours for a stronger taste. If available, vacuum pack at setting five and cure for 3 hours.

4. Heat 75 ml coconut or vegetable oil in frying pan until very hot. Quickly sear each fish fillet on each side for 15 seconds.

5. Place fillets into a smoker and smoke to a core temperature of 50°C.

SOUS VIDE COOKING

It is the process of cooking vacuum-sealed food at very tightly controlled temperatures.

How Sous Vide Works

Sous vide was first used in French kitchens in the 1970s. The term "sous vide" literally means "under vacuum". It is the process of cooking vacuum-sealed food at very tightly controlled temperatures. In contrast to traditional methods that cook food at high temperatures, sous vide cooks food at the temperature at which it will be served. This is why sous vide is also known as "low temperature cooking". With sous vide, many chefs are able to achieve the desired texture and doneness that is not possible with other cooking techniques.

The approach we have taken in this book is rather simple. Tender, delicate cuts require very gentle and precise cooking temperatures. This is why we recommend sous vide cooking mainly for chicken, beef steaks and seafood dishes. Secondary cuts from the neck, shoulder, ribs, tongue or shin that are rather tough and require much longer cooking times are best cooked in a pressure cooker (pages 21-22). Sous vide works like a pressure cooker in a sense that the sealed plastic bag prevents flavours from leaching out. It also avoids cross contamination. To understand the benefits of sous vide, it is important to know how different temperatures affect meat. At about 48°C, the connective tissues within the meat start to break down, resulting in tenderisation. If heat is increased, the tenderisation process increases as well. This is where we exercise caution, for above 60°C, collagen shrinks and wrings moisture from the meat, causing dryness and a tough texture. With sous vide cooking, the temperature can be controlled so that the meat does not dry out. Also, as the food is held in a sealed bag, it does not lose moisture or flavour. This is in sharp contrast to traditional cooking methods such as roasting or boiling, which often result in loss of fat and moisture. This, combined with the low temperature concept of sous vide, results in a very succulent and tender dish. While this is effective for meats that can dry out or toughen when cooked using the usual high heat methods, cooking using the sous vide method can take a very long time, often taking days. So, if you are willing to give it a try, note that most recipes often indicate cooking durations of 48–72 hours for tougher cuts of meat.

Sous Vide Equipment

The essentials for sous vide are a water bath, heat regulators and sous vide pouches. Most of the benefits of sous vide are due to the controlled and low temperature cooking process. This means that for those who are not willing to splurge on fancier tools such as vacuum sealers and other specialised equipment, there are cheaper alternatives. For example, a crockpot would work just as well as it can hold a relatively large amount of water. To help with regulating temperatures, a good digital thermometer can be used. And, instead of sous vide pouches, re-sealable waterproof plastic bags will suffice. Here are some readily available options:

1. A pot large enough for the food package to move about; a roomy self-heating device, such as a rice cooker or crockpot, is better as it maintains a more stable temperature
2. As an alternative to self-heating devices, a stovetop for heating a pot of water bath can be used instead
3. A good digital thermometer
4. Re-sealable waterproof plastic bags

Conclusion

It may sound strange to prepare ethnic Indonesian cuisine in plastic bags, as this is a distinct departure from the usual cooking techniques that many are accustomed to. However, if you enjoy experimenting with food and would like to enjoy the benefits of sous vide, I highly encourage you to venture in this new direction. You will see that in no time, you will master the basics of this incredible cooking technique and then not only you, but also your family and friends, will love the new tastes and flavours created by sous vide.

Basic Sous Vide Temperature Chart

These temperatures and times are based on tender prime cuts and are not for tough or secondary cuts that require much longer cooking times.

BEEF
Sirloin, tenderloin, rib eyes 20–30mm cut
Rare 50°C 20–25 minutes
Medium 55°C 30–40 minutes
Well done 60°C 40–60 minutes

Prime rib roast
Medium rare 55°C 5–10 hours
Medium 60°C 6–10 hours

Rib eye roast
Medium rare 55°C 5–10 hours
Medium 60°C 6–10 hours

Ribs
Medium 60°C 24–36 hours
Well done 71°C 24–36 hours

CHICKEN
Whole butterfly boneless 1.2-1.4 kg 65°C 40–60 minutes

Chicken leg, skinless, boneless, 20–30mm 65°C 40–60 minutes

FISH AND SEAFOOD
Fillets rare 50°C 15–20 minutes
Fillets medium 55°C 20–30 minutes
Prawns (shrimp) 55°C 25–30 minutes

Chicken in Spiced Coconut Sauce (*Opor Ayam*)

4 baby chickens, 750 g each, opened butterfly-style and completely deboned

100 ml vegetable or coconut oil

15 g palm sugar, chopped

375 ml chicken stock (page 44)

125 ml coconut cream

3 stalks lemongrass, bruised

2 salam leaves

3 kaffir lime leaves, bruised

salt, to taste

4 chicken eggs or 20 quail eggs

200 g potatoes, cut to your liking

1 stalk young leek, finely sliced

SPICE BLEND

1 Tbsp coriander seeds, roasted

1 tsp cumin, roasted

$^1/_2$ tsp crushed white pepper

2 Tbsp coconut oil

30 g galangal (*laos*), peeled and sliced

60 g shallots, peeled and sliced

30 g garlic, peeled and sliced

30 g candlenuts, roasted and crushed

1. Brine the chickens for 5 hours: refrigerate for the first 3 hours and then at room temperature for the remaining 2 hours (see page 32). Rinse the chickens thoroughly under running water and then dry with a kitchen towel.

2. Heat oil until smoking. Quickly sear each chicken for 30 seconds on each side until light golden colour. Set aside and allow oil to drain and allow chicken to cool.

3. To make the spice blend, combine coriander seeds, cumin and white peppercorns in a stone mortar or food processor and grind finely. Add all other ingredients and grind into a fine paste.

4. Heat 2 Tbsp oil in a heavy saucepan. Add spice paste and palm sugar and sauté until fragrant. Fill the saucepan with chicken stock and coconut cream. Add lemongrass, salam and kaffir lime leaves. Bring to a boil, then reduce heat and simmer for 5 minutes. Season to taste with salt. Allow the sauce to cool to room temperature.

5. Place each chicken individually into a heat resistant plastic bag. Fill each bag with equal amounts of sauce. Make certain not to wet the area of the bag that will be sealed. Vacuum seal and cook at 65°C for 40 minutes. Open each bag and pour the sauce into a saucepan and

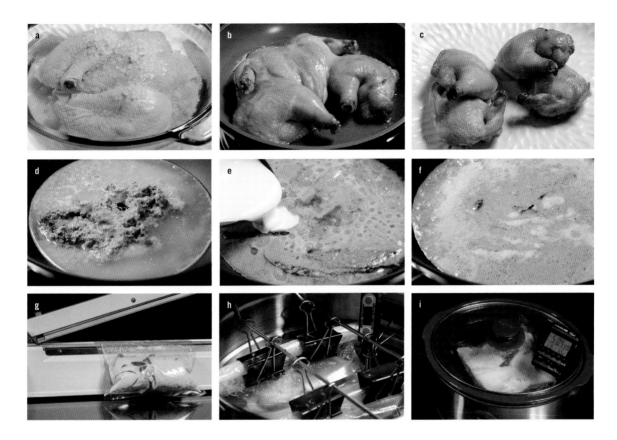

This has to be one of Central Java's most popular dishes that is prepared on a daily basis in everyone's home. Most ceremonies and royal banquets would not be complete without *opor ayam* as well. Looking at this recipe is a little like walking through a market in Central Java where each and every ingredient is plentiful including potatoes that are grown in large quantities at the Dieng Plateau, not far from Yogyakarta. Yes this version is a little more labour intensive and takes a longer time to prepare. However, the gentle usage of heat and a heatproof plastic bag will result in an incredibly tasty dish.

bring to a simmer. Season to taste with salt and some lime zest and lime juice. Using a hand blender, blend sauce for 15 seconds.

6. Place the eggs in a small pot of warm water. Cover and quickly bring to a boil. When the water comes to a boil, remove the pot from heat. Cover and wait for 3 minutes. Drain the water and plunge the eggs into ice water for 10 seconds. Do not allow the eggs to cool. Peel the eggs and add to the coconut sauce.

7. Wash the potatoes thoroughly. Place them into a saucepan, fill with warm water and a generous pinch of salt, then slowly boil the potatoes.

8. Cut the chickens into halves and arrange in a serving dish. Serve with eggs and potatoes. Pour the sauce over and around and garnish with finely sliced young leek.

NOTE
Should the sauce thicken too much, add small amounts of chicken stock. Serve with steamed rice (page 50) or rice cakes (page 173).

ESSENTIAL FLAVOURS OF INDONESIAN COOKING

SPICE BLENDS

A great Indian chef once remarked to me that in India, the flavour of curry blends changes every 50 kilometres. To me, this applies not only to India, but also to Indonesia and other parts of the world. It seems to me that the closer a region is to the equator, the more spices are used. This goes back to the days when there was no refrigeration and food had to be preserved using salt and spices.

In Indonesia, almost every cooking process starts in a stone mortar, with fresh spices ground into paste. As preparing spice blends is time-consuming, I would suggest preparing a larger quantity and keeping the blends in the freezer. Frozen spice blends will keep for months. Alternatively, you can also dry the spice blends, another age-old method of food preservation.

An affordable and effective way to dry food is to lay it in the sun and allow nature to do all the work. Drying spices in the sun takes about two full days. While it is a slow process, it yields the best results and retains much of the flavour and texture of the spices.

A ventilated chamber, a fan and a small heater that warms and dries the circulating air is also an inexpensive method. An oven set at the lowest possible temperature (around 60°C) will work too. It may be tempting to use a higher temperature to speed up the process, but higher temperatures will affect the quality of the spice blend.

The recipes below are for preparing spice blends. The process of making dry spice blends is exactly the same as making the paste version except no oil is added and the spices are dried until they reduce to a powder form.

Known as the Spice Islands in the far east of Indonesia, Maluku was obsessively sought for many years before they where rediscovered by Portuguese sailors in the 15th century. Explorers like Christopher Columbus, Vasco da Gama, Ferdinand Magellan and Sir Francis Drake all dreamt of seeking a fortune there. In fact, one of the main incentives for Europe's age of discovery was the avid search for spices, easily worth their weight in gold then. Spices like nutmeg, mace and cloves were used to camouflage the flavour of spoiled meat in the days long before refrigeration. It was also believed that these exotic spices had huge medicinal value. As far back as the 3rd century BC, the Chinese knew of cloves, and by the 4th century AD, fragrant cloves had reached Europe. Yet for hundreds of years, the world's total clove production came from five little islands in the far east of Indonesia, Ternate and Tidore in the north, Ambon in the centre and the island group of Banda on the southern edge of the spice islands. Control over these spice-producing islands assured one immeasurable fortune, and countless lives were lost in the quest to possess them. But the introduction of refrigeration and British success in propagating nutmeg and cloves in Sri Lanka was to end the spice wars for ever. Even more astonishing is the fact that these indigenous spices to Indonesia were actually introduced into Indonesian cooking by Indian traders.

Seafood Spice Blend
(*Bumbu Ikan*)

450 g large red chillies, seeded and sliced

20 g bird's eye chillies, finely sliced

220 g shallots, peeled and sliced

50 g garlic, peeled and sliced

175 g turmeric, peeled and sliced

100 g ginger, peeled and sliced

200 g tomatoes, grilled, peeled, halved and seeded, juice reserved

125 g candlenuts, crushed

2 Tbsp crushed coriander seeds

2 Tbsp dried shrimp (prawn) paste (*terasi*), roasted

¾ Tbsp salt

2 kaffir lime leaves, bruised

3 salam leaves

2 stalks lemongrass, bruised

150 ml coconut oil

4 Tbsp tamarind juice

250 ml water

Meat Spice Blend
(*Bumbu Daging*)

250 g large red chillies, halved, seeded and sliced

40 g bird's eye chillies, finely sliced

200 g shallots, peeled and sliced

50 g garlic, peeled and sliced

75 g ginger, peeled and sliced

75 g galangal (*laos*), peeled and chopped

75 g turmeric, peeled and sliced

100 g candlenut

1 tsp crushed black peppercorns

1 Tbsp crushed coriander seeds

40 g palm sugar, chopped

¾ Tbsp salt

3 salam leaves

150 ml coconut oil

250 ml water

Vegetable Spice Blend
(*Bumbu Sayur*)

250 g large red chillies halved, seeded and sliced

25 g bird's eye chillies, sliced

100 g shallots, peeled and sliced

100 g garlic, peeled and sliced

75 g galangal (*laos*), peeled and thinly sliced

75 g fresh turmeric, peeled and sliced

50 g lesser galangal (*kencur*), washed and sliced

75 g ginger, peeled and sliced

100 g candlenuts

1 Tbsp crushed coriander seeds

1 tsp white crushed peppercorns

¾ Tbsp salt

2 salam leaves

2 stalks lemongrass, bruised

150 ml vegetable oil

250 ml water

Fresh Spice Blend

1. Combine all ingredients except tamarind juice, kaffir lime leaves, salam leaves, lemongrass, oil and water in a food processor or stone mortar. Grind until fine.

2. Transfer ground ingredients to a pressure cooker and add remaining ingredients. Bring to a simmer.

3. Pressure cook at 15 psi for 30 minutes (see pages 21-22). Start timing when full pressure is reached. Leave the cooker to cool for 20 minutes before opening.

4. Refrigerate spice paste overnight, then place chilled spice paste into an ice cube tray and freeze. Store frozen spice paste cubes in an airtight container in the freezer and use as needed.

NOTE

You can use this same process to prepare individual spices such as chillies. Halve and seed the chillies before grinding them finely.

Dry Spice Blend

1. Follow the same directions for the fresh spice paste blend but without using oil. Once cooked, spread the paste on a tray in a layer no more than 0.5-cm thick and leave to dry.

2. Stir the spice paste thoroughly with a fork every hour to ensure even drying. Once completely dry, finely purée or, better yet, blend in a coffee grinder.

3. Store in an airtight container or glass jar with a small food-safe silicon pack to keep dry.

STOCKS

Stocks can add a lot of flavour and character to a dish. To make a stock with a good balance of flavours, we need to take note of the five basic tastes. Good seasoning can take a dish to the next level.

LIGHT STOCK

A soup stock should be as clear and tasty as possible because it forms the base for dishes.

1. Remove fat from bones and meat. Wash thoroughly.
2. Place bones and meat in a pot of cold water and bring to a quick boil. This step helps to remove impurities and coagulate proteins so the resultant stock is not cloudy.
3. Drain and rinse the bones and meat thoroughly. Place in a pot and add water. The ratio of water to bones and meat should be 3:1 respectively. Simmer for 5–6 hours.

DARK STOCK

Dark stocks are used typically for brown sauces. The bones are roasted golden in a medium-hot oven to produce colour and a more intense, meaty flavour that is the result of Maillard reactions.

Within our kitchens, all our stocks are prepared in a pressure cooker. To intensify the flavour, two-thirds of the bones are blanched and the remaining third is roasted golden. Towards the end of the roasting process, a small amount of full-cream milk powder, which is also roasted golden, will be added to the stock.

HOW TO PRESSURE COOK STOCKS

The pressure cooker is a great way to prepare stocks, as not only does it retain all the flavour, if used correctly, it can yield stocks that are nearly as clear as a consommé. Although this method takes three days, the outcome is well worth it. All you need is a pressure cooker, some extra space in a deep freezer and a passion for good food. With proper planning, the process can be very simple.

1. Grind meat and slice vegetables as thinly as possible.
2. Use minimal heat.
3. Roast bones, meat or other sources of gelatin in oven. If desired, reserve 10% of raw ground meat for a clearer stock.
4. Brown meat in fat directly in the cooker. Oven browning is also acceptable, but browning in the cooker is more flavourful. Remove meat after it is just browned and not too dark in colour. Be careful not to scorch or over-brown the meat as this will produce a bitter taste. Add vegetables and cook until soft. Remove vegetables and deglaze the base from any excess juices. If needed, deglaze further with water or other liquids, such as wine.

5. Return browned meat and vegetables to the pot. Add remaining ingredients, such as liquids, roasted bones, optional aromatics and optional reserved ground meat.

6. Bring to a simmer and skim off the scum.

7. Cover and bring to full pressure, then reduce heat to an absolute minimum to maintain pressure. Pressure cook at 15 psi without venting. The cooker should not whistle, as this would mean the stock is boiling. Take care not to let the contents boil while the stock simmers. Boiling not only stresses the equipment but also causes turbulence that emulsifies the fats and turns the stock cloudy.

8. Remove from heat and cool until the pressure abates. You can accelerate cooling by running cold water over the pot.

9. The solids should have sunk to the bottom with a layer of oil at the top and a thin layer of buoyant particles just below the oil. Skim off the fat and strain the stock. Leave the solids at the bottom as you decant the stock. To get an even clearer stock, use a siphon. You can also chill the stock to solidify the fat. Once the layer of fat solidifies, make a hole through it and pour out the stock.

Umami and Indonesian Cooking

Umami was unknown to many early cooks. It was discovered by Professor Ikeda of the University of Tokyo. He discovered it in the early 1900s when he investigated the properties of konbu, a giant kelp used to flavour Japanese dishes, particularly for dashi, a stock. The savoury taste that konbu imparts to dashi comes from its glutamic acid. This discovery led Professor Ikeda to develop a commercial version of that glutamic acid, which he called monosodium glutamate, or MSG.

So how does this relate to Indonesian cooking? As most rural areas do not have refrigerators, meat must be prepared the same day as the animals are slaughtered. Most Indonesians will boil the meat in water or coconut milk for hours along with spices. To finish the dish, a large pinch of sugar or MSG is added for that crucial umami taste. This method, however, often makes the dish very oily. The recipes in this book for such authentic dishes as the Padang beef rendang are tweaked to reduce the oiliness and improve the flavour. The amount of coconut milk used has been reduced and stock, which will also add to the essential umami flavour, is used as well. As the stock ingredients are rich in natural umami, it is not necessary to add MSG.

Basic Indonesian Chicken/Duck/Beef Stock (*Kuah Indonesia*)

6 kg chicken or duck or beef bones without skin and fat, cut into 2.5-cm pieces or smaller

150 g meat spice paste

2 stalks lemongrass, bruised

2 kaffir lime leaves, torn

2 large red chillies, bruised

3-5 bird's eye chillies

2 salam leaves

½ tsp coarsely crushed black peppercorns

½ tsp crushed coriander seeds

Day 1

1. Rinse bones until water runs clear. Transfer to a stockpot and cover with cold water. Bring to a boil over high heat to blanch the bones. Drain and discard water.

2. Rinse bones again and return half the bones to a larger stockpot, reserving the other half for the next day.

3. Add three times as much water as bones and bring to a boil. Lower the heat and skim off any scum as it accumulates.

4. Add all ingredients. Seal the pressure cooker and cook at 1 bar/15 psi for 2 hours (see pages 21-22). Start timing as soon as full pressure has been reached.

5. Remove from heat and cool until the pressure abates. You can accelerate cooling by running cold water over the pot.

6. Strain the liquid and discard the solids. Set aside to cool for use the next day.

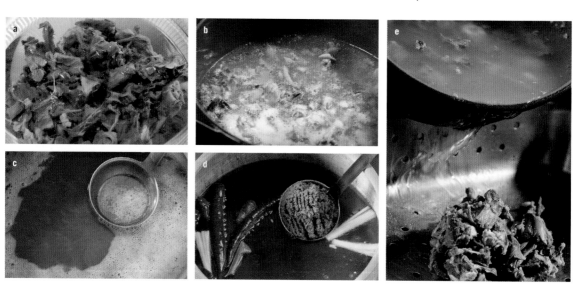

Day 2

1. Fill stockpot with the reserved bones and stock prepared from day 1. Bring to a boil.

2. Strain the liquid and discard the solids. Set aside to cool before freezing it. Depending on your freezer, the stock should freeze in 2–3 days.

Day 3

1. Line a large fine strainer with cheesecloth. Place it over a deep container large enough to contain the consommé without the strainer touching the bottom of the pot.

2. Place the frozen stock in the strainer and let it thaw in the refrigerator. This may take up to 2 days.

3. Collect the resultant consommé and discard the fat and larger particles left in the strainer.

The Five Basic Tastes

- Saltiness helps add taste to food, and it is easily achieved by adding salt.

- Sweetness makes food taste pleasant, and is easily achieved by adding sugar.

- Sourness can help balance out flavours in food, and in Asian dishes, it can come from sources such as tamarind or limes.

- Bitterness, like sourness, can help bring out the flavour of other ingredients, and it can come from the usage of a variety of roots, like ginger, galangal or turmeric.

- Umami has been considered the fifth basic taste since the early 1900s. It is a Japanese term that means "pleasant, savoury taste" and is used to describe something tasty that cannot quite be categorised as salty, sweet, sour or bitter.

Seafood Stock (*Kaldu Udang*)

1 kg seafood shells (lobster, prawns, crabs or crayfish)

3 Tbsp coconut oil

150 g seafood spice blend (page 51)

2 stalks lemongrass, bruised

3 kaffir lime leaves, crushed

2 large red chillies

4-6 bird's eye chillies

2 litres water or preferably light chicken stock (page 44)

1. Clean the seafood shells and discard any organs, including the gills and eyes. Chop or crush shells with a heavy knife or cleaver. Smaller pieces infuse more flavour into the stock.

2. Heat coconut oil in the base of a pressure cooker and sauté the shells for 6–8 minutes until light golden brown.

3. Add seafood spice blend, lemongrass, kaffir lime leaves and chillies. Sauté for another 2 minutes.

4. Deglaze with 250 ml water or stock and sauté for another 2 minutes.

5. Add remaining water or stock and bring to a boil. Skim off any scum.

6. Cook at 15 psi for 1 hour (see pages 21-22). Start timing once full pressure is reached. Leave the cooker to cool for 30 minutes before opening.

7. Strain the stock through a sieve lined with cheesecloth.

NOTE
Whenever you prepare crustaceans, save the shells in the freezer until you have enough to make a stock. Alternatively, use inexpensive whole prawns.

Vegetable Stock (*Kaldu Sayur*)

3 fresh ears of corn, shucked, husk reserved

3 Tbsp coconut oil

150 g vegetable spice blend (page 52)

3 kaffir lime leaves, bruised

2 stalks lemongrass, bruised

100 g shallots, peeled and thinly sliced

200 g carrots, peeled and thinly sliced into matchsticks

100 g celery with leaves, thinly sliced

100 g leek, finely sliced

50 g shiitake mushrooms, finely sliced

100 g tomatoes, halved and sliced

100 g pumpkin, peeled and thinly sliced into matchsticks

2 litres water

1. Preheat the oven to 175°C.

2. Cut the corn into short lengths. Shred the cornhusk and scatter it with the corn pieces on a baking tray. Invert a cooling rack on the corn and husk to hold them in place. Bake for about 20 minutes or until golden brown, turning the corn over once or twice during baking.

3. Heat the coconut oil in a pressure cooker and add the spice blend, kaffir lime leaves and lemongrass. Sauté for 2 minutes until fragrant.

4. Add the baked corn and husk and remaining ingredients except water. Sauté for 5 minutes over medium heat.

5. Add the water and bring to a boil. Skim off any scum.

6. Pressure cook at 15 psi for 45 minutes (see pages 21-22). Start timing once full pressure is reached. Leave the cooker to cool for 30 minutes before opening.

7. Strain the stock through a sieve lined with cheesecloth.

NOTE

For a brown vegetable stock, toss the ingredients together with the corn in 3 Tbsp coconut oil, then roast in a 220°C-oven until golden brown. Cook as above.

RICE

Every Indonesian eats 380 g of rice per day. Rice is central to Indonesian cuisine, and a large part of the Indonesian population is involved in rice farming.

I find it absolutely astonishing that the many guests I meet in our restaurants and during our cooking classes have difficulty cooking perfectly fluffy and tasty rice. If you consider that two-thirds of the world's population depends on rice as a main source for carbohydrates then preparing rice cannot be all that difficult. I therefore find it essential to explain here the various steps in detail, this is to ensure that from now on, you will always be able to prepare perfect cooked rice for your loved ones. Obviously there are countless ways to so, but we will stick to the two most popular methods found throughout Indonesia: steamed over a pot of boiling water cooked to perfection in an inexpensive rice cooker. And then of course we will look at various ways to make rice an absolutely essential component in your next perfect meal.

White rice

Red rice

Black rice

Rice is central to Indonesian cuisine, and a large part of the Indonesian population is involved in rice farming. Long-grained rice is typically eaten during meals, while glutinous or sticky rice is usually used for desserts, cakes and rice wine. Black rice is also used for making cakes, wines and offerings.

Most Indonesians use the words "rice" and "food" interchangeably. An invitation to eat is commonly phrased as, "Let's go have rice." Steamed rice, or *nasi kuskus*, is most often eaten with side dishes such as vegetables and meat. There are also various types of flavoured rice, such as *nasi uduk* (coconut milk rice), *nasi kuning* (coconut milk and turmeric rice) and *nasi goreng* (fried rice). Other forms of rice products include vermicelli and *arak beras* (rice wine).

Steamed White Rice (*Nasi Putih*) or Red Rice (*Nasi Merah*)

375 g long grain rice
750 ml boiling water

Steamer method

1. Wash and rinse rice well, then soak in fresh water for 25 minutes.

2. Drain rice and transfer to the steamer. Steam for 20–25 minutes.

3. Transfer rice to a deep bowl and fluff it up using two spoons.

4. Add boiling water and leave for 5 minutes until the rice absorbs the water.

5. Return rice to the steamer and steam for another 20–25 minutes or until rice is tender. Fluff up rice to allow excess moisture to evaporate.

6. Lower the heat and keep rice warm in the steamer until ready to serve

375 g long grain rice
500 ml cold water

Rice cooker method

1. Wash and rinse rice well, then soak in fresh water for 25 minutes.

2. Drain rice and transfer to a rice cooker.

3. Add cold water. (Note that the ratio of rice to water is 1:1.5 respectively.)

4. Leave rice to cook.

Yellow Rice (*Nasi Kuning*)

250 g long grain rice, washed and drained

DRESSING

1 Tbsp coconut oil

50 g shallots, peeled and chopped

25 g garlic, peeled and chopped

1 stalk lemongrass, bruised

2 salam leaves

1 stalk pandan leaf, bruised

375 ml vegetable or chicken stock

60 ml turmeric water, from grinding
    2.5-cm knob chopped turmeric with
    water until very fine, then straining it

125 ml coconut milk

Salt, to taste

Ground white pepper, to taste

NOTE

To prepare a lighter version of nasi kuning, replace coconut milk with an addtional 125 ml stock.

Steamer method

1. Wash and rinse rice well, then soak in fresh water for 25 minutes.

2. Drain rice and transfer to a conventional steamer. Steam for 20–25 minutes.

3. Meanwhile, prepare the dressing. Heat oil in a saucepan. Add shallots and garlic and sauté for 1 minute. Add lemongrass, salam leaves and pandan leaf. Sauté for another minute. Add stock and turmeric water. Bring to a boil, then lower the heat to simmer for 1 minute. Add coconut milk and bring to a boil, then lower the heat to simmer for 2 minutes. Season to taste with salt and pepper.

4. Transfer steamed rice into a deep bowl and add dressing. Mix well and allow rice to absorb the liquid.

5. Return rice to the steamer and steam for another 25 minutes or until rice is tender.

Rice cooker method

1. Prepare dressing as above and leave to cool.

2. Wash and rinse rice well, then soak in fresh water for 25 minutes.

3. Drain and transfer rice to a rice cooker. Mix in cooled dressing.

4. Leave rice to cook until tender.

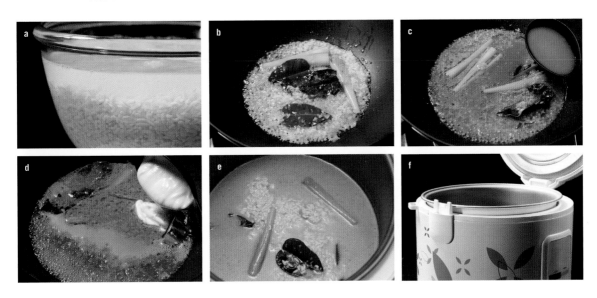

CONDIMENTS

GREAT LITTLE CONDIMENTS OF INDONESIA

Many guests in our restaurants often approach me with a request to prepare dishes that are not spicy.

It is a common misconception amongst visitors to Indonesia that food throughout this massive country is spicy and that every dish is prepared with excessive amounts of chilli. Nothing could be further from the truth. It is not the dish itself that is spicy, it is the condiment.

During my numerous travels across Indonesia, I visited many areas that rarely use chillies in their cooking, as they were not grown there. Instead, very mild dishes are produced that would definitely suit a Western palate.

The same can be said about Balinese cooking, which has the unwarranted reputation of being fiery hot. Whenever I tell Balinese people that I cook Balinese food for a living, they automatically ask me if I can eat spicy food and whether the dishes I prepare are as spicy as those prepared in a Balinese home. The answer, of course, is 'yes' and not only at home but also in our restaurants. However, I also point out that not all Balinese dishes are spicy. Perhaps the most famous Balinese dish is *babi guling*, which is definitely not spicy, and the same applies to Balinese *satays*. So how did the myth that Balinese or Indonesian food is spicy originate?

The answer lies in the condiments that are always served on the side, together with the dishes in the centre of the table. These condiments can be fiercely hot, and this is what has given Balinese and Indonesian food the reputation of being very spicy cuisine.

To do justice to the great condiments of Indonesian and Balinese cuisine, I have dedicated an entire section in this book to them. I should point out that it does not matter whether you serve a dish that originates from Maluku with a Sumatran condiment. A grilled chicken from Lombok tastes sensational when served with yellow pickles from Flores and a baked tomato sambal from West Sumatra. We also highly recommend that you serve these great condiments not just as part of your next Indonesian meal but also consider them for your next barbecue of Western-style grilled fish or steaks.

Peanut Sauce *(Base Satay)* *Bali*

In most tourist hotels and restaurants, this sauce is served together with *satay* as a dipping sauce. The Balinese themselves would never serve a dipping sauce with their *satay*, but instead provide a condiment of salt and chopped chillies. Nevertheless, we cannot publish a book on Indonesian cuisine without including peanut sauce. The sauce is not used for meat dishes but as a dipping sauce for vegetables.

500 g raw peanuts with skin, deep-fried or roasted golden brown

5 garlic cloves, peeled and sliced

8-10 bird's eye chillies, finely sliced

10 g ginger, peeled and very finely sliced

10 g galangal (*laos*), peeled and finely sliced

1 litre coconut milk

20 g palm sugar, chopped

4 Tbsp sweet soy sauce (*kecap manis*)

2 kaffir lime leaves, torn

1 Tbsp lime juice

1 Tbsp fried shallots

salt, to taste

1. Combine peanuts, garlic, chillies, ginger and galangal in a food processor or stone mortar and grind finely.

2. Place ground ingredients in a heavy saucepan together with three-quarters coconut milk, palm sugar and sweet soy sauce. Bring to a boil, then reduce heat and simmer uncovered for 10 minutes, stirring frequently to prevent the sauce from sticking. Should the sauce become too thick, add the remaining coconut milk and, if necessary, a little more water.

3. Add lime juice and sprinkle with shallots just before serving as a dipping sauce for satay. Season to taste with salt.

NOTE
It is almost impossible to precisely define the amount of coconut milk or water needed in a recipe. Every time we prepare this sauce, the quantities used will vary slightly. Do the same at home and gradually add more liquid as needed.

Chilli Tomato Sauce *(Sambal Lombok)* *Flores*

Indonesians love chillies in their food and often use what would be considered an excessive amount by Western standards. Chillies grow in Indonesia and come in many colours, shapes and sizes. They can be as tiny as a baby's finger or as long as 20 cm. When buying chillies, check that they are very firm to the touch, shiny, smooth-skinned, and the stems must be green or red, and crunchy. It is best to use chillies immediately after they have been harvested and avoid storing them for extended periods in the refrigerator as this will intensify their spiciness and change their natural, crisp, clean flavour and aroma. The Indonesian cook mostly uses three types of chillies with the level of spiciness inversely increasing with the decreasing size of the chilli. Always wear gloves when handling chillies; wash your hands and all surfaces that have come into contact with the chillies.

75 ml coconut oil

100 g shallots, peeled and sliced

20 g garlic, peeled and sliced

200 g large red chillies, halved, seeded and sliced

50 g bird's eye chillies

2 Tbsp sweet soy sauce (*kecap manis*)

¹/₂ tsp dried prawn (shrimp) paste (*terasi*), roasted

200 g tomatoes, roasted, peeled and seeded

salt, to taste

2 Tbsp lime juice

1. Heat oil in a heavy saucepan over moderate high heat.

2. Add shallots and garlic and sauté until golden.

3. Add chillies and continue to sauté until chillies become soft.

4. Add sweet soy sauce and prawn paste, and continue to sauté for 2 minutes.

5. Add tomatoes and continue to sauté until tomatoes are soft. Set aside to cool.

6. Grind in a stone mortar or purée coarsely in food processor.

7. Season to taste with salt and lime juice.

NOTE

Make certain to cook all ingredients over high heat while continually mixing. This will preserve the nice, crisp, red colour of the mixture.

To peel the tomatoes, quickly roast them over an open gas flame or over a barbecue, which will make it easier to remove the skins. The smoky flavour that the tomatoes then develop adds a pleasant aroma and is especially tasty when served with grilled seafood.

Spiced Tomato Sauce *(Saus Pedas Tomat)* West Sumatra

Anything grilled tastes delicious with this sauce. The amount of bird's eye chillies specified in this recipe is only an indication of how we like the sauce: mildly spicy. Add more chillies for a spicier sauce.

150 g large red chillies, halved, seeded and sliced

5-7 bird's eye chillies, finely sliced

20 g ginger, peeled, sliced and finely chopped

75 g shallots, peeled and sliced

20 g garlic, peeled and sliced

3 Tbsp coconut or vegetable oil

2 kaffir lime leaves, bruised

1 salam leaf

60 g red onions, peeled and finely chopped

150 g tomato, grilled, peeled, halved, seeded and diced (keep liquid)

1 Tbsp oyster sauce

salt, to taste

2 Tbsp lime juice

1. Combine chillies, ginger, shallots and garlic in a stone mortar or food processor and grind into a very fine paste.

2. Heat oil in a saucepan. Add ground spices, lime and salam leaves and sauté for 1 minute until fragrant. Add onions and continue to sauté over medium heat for 2 more minutes.

3. Add tomatoes and oyster sauce, mix well and sauté for another 2 minutes.

4. Add tomato juice from the seeds and bring back to a simmer.

5. Season to taste with salt and lime juice.

Spicy Chilli Sauce *(Sambal Pedas)* *Flores*

Prepare this delicate but fiery sauce as and when it is needed. If prepared in advance, the fragrance of the lime juice and lemon basil will quickly dissipate. The sauce tastes just as delicious when prepared with green chillies as seen in the photo.

100 g large red chillies, halved, seeded and sliced

100 g bird's eye chillies, sliced

50 g shallots, peeled and sliced

1 pinch salt + more to taste

2 Tbsp lime juice

3 Tbsp roughly chopped lemon basil (*kemangi*)

1. Combine chillies, shallots and salt in a stone mortar or food processor and grind into a fine paste.

2. Add lime juice and lemon basil and grind again for an additional $1/2$ minute.

3. Season to taste with salt.

Almond Sauce *(Sambal Kenari)* *Maluku*

A terrific dressing with grilled-smoked fish or meats, or as a basic dressing for a tasty vegetable salad, *sambal kenari* is a very popular condiment on the island of Ternate of the Spice Islands.

50 g shallots, peeled and sliced

3-5 bird's eye chillies, finely sliced

100 g almonds, blanched and peeled

100 g tomatoes, grilled, peeled, seeded and diced

2 Tbsp sliced lemon basil (*kemangi*)

2 Tbsp lime juice

salt, to taste

1. Combine shallots, chillies and almonds in a stone mortar or food processor and grind into a coarse paste.

2. Add tomatoes and lemon basil and grind to mix. Season to taste with lime juice and salt.

Chilli Shallot Dressing *(Sambal Rica Kering)* *Moluku*

Addictive with grilled fish and meats, the flavour really develops when blended with a generous helping of steamed rice.

6 Tbsp coconut oil

100 g shallots, peeled and sliced

100 g large red chillies, halved, seeded and finely sliced

7-9 bird's eye chillies, finely sliced (add more if you like it very spicy)

2 stalks lemongrass, bruised, very finely sliced and then chopped

1 Tbsp turmeric water (very concentrated, see page 61)

salt, to taste

1. In the frying pan, heat the oil until smoking. Add shallots and fry until golden.

2. Add chillies and lemongrass and continue to fry for 1 more minute over high heat.

3. Add turmeric water and fry for another 30 seconds.

4. Remove from heat and season to taste with salt.

Shallot and Lemon Grass Dressing *(Sambal Matah)* *Bali*

Another way to make this delicious dressing is to heat the oil in a saucepan, then cook all ingredients for 5 minutes over medium heat, or until the sauce is fragrant. Let it cool to room temperature before serving. Blend *sambal matah* and *sambal tomat* from Bali and serve with grilled fish.

100 g shallots, peeled, cut into halves and finely sliced

100 g lemongrass, bruised, finely sliced and chopped

30 g bird's eye chillies, finely sliced

2 kaffir lime leaves, finely chopped

1/2 tsp finely crumbled prawn (shrimp) cake, roasted

2 Tbsp lime juice

4 Tbsp coconut oil

salt and pepper, to taste

1. Combine the ingredients in a deep bowl and mix thoroughly for 5 minutes.

2. Season to taste with salt and pepper.

Shallot-turmeric Coconut Cream Dressing *(Sambal Acar) Moluku*

This dressing is delicious with grilled fish and addictive with smoked fish.

150 g shallots, peeled and sliced
60 ml coconut cream
200 ml seafood stock (page 46)
50 ml turmeric water
2 Tbsp lime juice
salt, to taste

1. Combine shallots, coconut cream, seafood stock and turmeric water in a saucepan and simmer over very light heat until sauce lightly thickens.

2. Season to taste with lime juice and salt.

NOTE
To make turmeric water, combine ½ water and ½ turmeric peeled and finely sliced in a food processor or stone mortar and grind into a fine paste. Strain the paste through a fine sieve.

Yellow Chilli Sambal *(Lombok Kuning) South Sulawesi*

This unique condiment goes well with a hearty beef soup. A key ingredient is carrot and the ingredients are first boiled in chicken stock.

1 litre chicken stock (page 44)
300 g large red chillies, halved, seeded and sliced
50 g bird's eye chillies, whole
150 g garlic, peeled and sliced
150 g carrots, cut into halves and finely sliced
1 tsp white sugar
salt, to taste
2 Tbsp lime juice

1. Bring chicken stock to a boil in a saucepan. Add chillies, garlic and carrots, and continue to simmer until ingredients are soft.

2. Purée in a food processor into a smooth sauce.

3. Pour sauce back into saucepan, bring to a boil and simmer until sauce lightly thickens.

4. Season to taste with sugar, salt and lime juice.

Green Tomato Anchovy Sauce *(Sambal Hijau)* West Sumatra

If you are reluctant to use dried anchovies or have difficulties finding them, then simply remove them from this simple recipe. However, if you are a big fan of this type of sun-dried seafood, then I would highly recommend giving it a go for this particular recipe. The flavour of crispy, fried tiny anchovies comes through very subtly and elevates the taste of the sauce. Keep in mind that dried anchovies are very high in umami and adds a tremendous amount of flavour. The sauce is delicious with grilled fish and many kinds of stews. If green chillies and green tomatoes are not available, replace with red ones and follow the same preparation.

100 g large green chillies

5-7 small green chillies

50 g shallots, peeled

40 g garlic, peeled

100 g green tomatoes

$^1/_2$ tsp dried prawn (shrimp) paste (*terasi*), roasted

salt, to taste

black pepper, crushed to taste

2 Tbsp lime juice

50 g dried anchovies, deep-fried until crisp

1. Combine chillies, shallots, garlic and tomato and steam for 10 minutes.

2. Cut large chillies lengthwise into halves and remove seeds and skin of tomatoes.

3. Place steamed ingredients into a stone mortar or food processor and grind coarsely.

4. Add prawn paste and blend well.

5. Season to taste with salt, pepper and lime juice.

6. Garnish with dried anchovies.

Baked Tomato Sambal *(Sambal Tomat)* *South Sumatra*

Incredibly tasty, not too spicy and with a balanced sweetness that works so well with any type of grilled foods, this has to be one of the best tomato *sambals* that I have sampled in Indonesia. Fish, prawns, chicken or even beef steaks taste better with this delectable sauce.

5 Tbsp coconut oil

20 g garlic, peeled and sliced

60 g large red chillies, halved, seeded and sliced

5-7 bird's eye chillies, sliced

$1/4$ tsp salt + more to taste

40 g shallots, peeled and sliced

100 g cherry tomatoes, peeled and halved

2 Tbsp sweet soy sauce (*kecap manis*)

1 Tbsp lime juice

30 g dried anchovies, deep-fried until crisp

1. Combine 2 Tbsp coconut oil, garlic, chillies and $1/4$ tsp of salt in a stone mortar or food processor and grind into a very fine paste.

2. Add the remaining coconut oil into a frying pan and heat. Add shallots and ground spices and sauté for 2 minutes over moderate heat until fragrant.

3. Add tomatoes and continue to sauté until tomatoes are soft and well cooked.

4. Add sweet soy sauce, lime juice, and season to taste with salt.

5. Just before serving, add dried anchovies and mix well.

Vegetable Dressing *(Sambal Pelecing)* *Lombok*

This is a terrific dressing that complements any green vegetables, including water spinach, spinach, fern tips, bean sprouts, green beans or any other greens that may need a flavour boost.

6-8 bird's eye chillies, finely sliced

2 medium-sized tomatoes, grilled, skin removed and seeded

$1/2$ Tbsp dried prawn (shrimp) paste, roasted

salt, to taste

75 ml vegetable or chicken stock (page 47 or 44)

1. Combine all ingredients in a stone mortar or food processor and grind into a paste. Season to taste with salt and adjust stock if necessary.

Pickled Vegetables (Acar Mentah) *Flores*

Vegetables are never eaten on their own except as accompaniments to rice, and they are never eaten raw. People of Flores do not eat salads of raw vegetables except for slices of raw cucumber. Few homes have refrigeration and there would be no way to keep raw vegetables fresh for any length of time. Vegetables are always eaten well-cooked and limp or soft. As with all accompaniments to rice, vegetables are usually put in a separate dish and placed next to the cooked rice. People prefer to eat them warm, but they often do not because they eat whenever they choose to, since there is no set meal time.

200 g cucumbers, peeled, halved, seeded and diced

200 g carrots, peeled and sliced into matchstick- sized pieces

100 g long beans, sliced into 3-cm lengths

100 g green mango, peeled and sliced

100 g pineapple, peeled and diced

50 g shallots, peeled and quartered

10 bird's eye chillies, whole

DRESSING

250 ml (1 cup) white vinegar (rice, wine or cider)

250 ml (1 cup) water

250 g white sugar

50 g ginger, peeled and crushed

2 stalks lemongrass, bruised

salt, to taste

1. To make the dressing, combine all the ingredients in a heavy saucepan. Bring to a boil, then reduce heat and simmer for 5 minutes. Set aside and cool.

2. Combine the remaining ingredients and dressing and marinate in the refrigerator for 24 hours.

Tomato Chilli Dressing (Sambal Tomat Mentah) *Maluku*

Adjust the level of spiciness by adding as many or as few small chillies to suit your liking.

6 Tbsp coconut oil

100 g shallots, peeled and sliced

4-7 bird's eye chillies, finely sliced

200 g tomatoes, grilled, peeled, seeded and diced

4 Tbsp lime juice

salt, to taste

1. Heat oil until very hot in a frying pan.

2. Add shallots, chillies and tomatoes and mix well. Remove pan from heat.

3. Add lime juice and season to taste with salt.

Tomato Sambal with Petai and Anchovies

(Sambal Lado Tanak) *West Sumatra*

Many people find petai beans smelly and horrible tasting, while the smell and flavour of dried anchovies (*ikan bilis*) have been described as akin to dead fish. However, once you have tried fresh petai beans and dried anchovies and looked at some of the nutritional facts, you will have lots of fun experimenting with these two unusual ingredients.

Research has proven that just two servings of petai provide enough energy for a strenuous 90-minute workout. Petai also helps to overcome or prevent a substantial number of illnesses and conditions, and is a must for the health-conscious.

150 g shallots, peeled and sliced

30 g garlic, peeled and sliced

250 g large red chillies, halved, seeded and sliced

5-7 bird's eye chillies, finely sliced

3 Tbsp coconut oil

100 g petai beans, blanched

375 ml chicken or vegetable stock (page 44 or 47)

125 ml coconut cream

100 g dried anchovies, deep-fried until crisp

salt, to taste

1. Combine shallots, garlic and chillies in a stone mortar or food processor and grind into a very fine paste.

2. Heat oil in a saucepan, add ground paste and sauté over medium heat until fragrant.

3. Add petai beans, stock and coconut cream and simmer paste to a creamy consistency.

4. Add dried anchovies, blend well and season to taste with salt.

SALADS

Vegetable and Almond Salad *(Sambal Ulang Ulang)* *Maluku*

1 medium eggplant, finely sliced

70 g green beans, sliced 2-cm long

70 g bean sprouts

1 medium cucumber, peeled, seeded
    and sliced

salt, to taste

ground white pepper, to taste

DRESSING

1 cup almond sauce (page 59)

100 g shallots, peeled and finely sliced

2 medium tomatoes, sliced

4 Tbsp finely sliced lemon basil *(kemangi)*

3 Tbsp lime juice

1. Bring a pot of water to the boil and blanch eggplant briefly until just tender. Set aside in a colander to drain.

2. Repeat to blanch green beans for about 2 minutes until tender but still crisp. Blanch bean sprouts for 15 seconds. Drain well.

3. Combine all ingredients for the dressing and mix well.

4. Combine the vegetables in a bowl and drizzle with the dressing. Toss well and season to taste with salt and white pepper. Serve.

The Sultan's Betel-nut-chewing Chefs

In our search for traditional dishes from the Spice Islands, we were fortunate enough to engage five private cooks from the Sultan of Ternate. Together they offered over 150 years of experience in preparing the finest dishes for royalty. One dish after another appeared in front of me as I noted down all the ingredients as well as the preparation of the dishes. Photographs were taken of the dishes to record their presentation and colours. Each dish was a work of art and a symphony of flavours. Each dish was different and as I sampled them, I found myself wanting to include my own finishing touch: a little more salt here and a little more pepper there, a squeeze of lime juice in the soup and perhaps a little more chilli in the chicken stew. In accordance with royal custom, the chefs refused to join our table to enjoy the fruits of their hard labour, as this would break a centuries-old tradition. Instead, they sat outside the kitchen chitchatting and chewing betel nuts. This obviously explains the lack of finishing touches in each dish, as I strongly believe that the taste buds of the chefs have been greatly affected by the acid found in the betel nuts.

Dried Fish and Tomato Salad *(Ikan Kering)* *Flores*

If dried fish is not to your taste, serve the dressing together with grilled or pan-fried seafood. However, I would highly recommend making an effort to prepare this very tasty and rather unusual seafood salad. It can be enjoyed as a salad or as a main meal with a generous helping of steamed rice.

300 g dried medium-sized fish
rice flour to dust fish for frying
oil for frying fish
ground white pepper, to taste

DRESSING
4 Tbsp vegetable oil
60 g shallots, peeled and sliced
200 g tomatoes, peeled, halved, seeded, sliced or diced
1 Tbsp palm sugar
5-7 bird's eye chillies, finely sliced
1 Tbsp tamarind water
2 Tbsp lime juice
4 Tbsp lemon basil (*kemangi*), roughly chopped
salt, to taste
ground white pepper, crushed to taste

1. Dust fish evenly with rice flour.

2. Deep-fry fish very slowly at 140°C–150°C until golden and very crispy. Make certain the heat increases very slowly during the frying process. Drain on absorbent paper towels.

3. To make the dressing, heat vegetable oil in a frying pan, add shallots and sauté until fragrant. Remove from heat and cool.

4. Add all other ingredients and blend well. Season to taste with salt and white crushed pepper.

5. In a deep mixing bowl, combine fish and dressing and blend well. Season to taste with white ground pepper.

6. Garnish as desired. Serve.

NOTE
To make tamarind water, dissolve 1 Tbsp tamarind pulp in 3 Tbsp warm water and strain.

Prawn and Squid Salad with Lime and Mint

(Dojang Nakeng) *Flores*

We discovered this seafood dish in the provincial town of Ruteng, 140 km inland.
The surprising use of mint in the dish was a first for us in Indonesia. Any type
of seafood or even beef and chicken can be used following the directions below.

1 litre seafood stock (page 46)

150 g seafood spice blend (page 40)

2 stalks lemongrass, bruised

3 kaffir lime leaves, bruised

500 g large prawns still in their shells,
brined in iced seafood brine for 2 hours
(see page 32)

300 g squid, cleaned and sliced

salt, to taste

ground white pepper, to taste

DRESSING

60 g shallots, peeled and finely sliced

2 large red chillies, halved, seeded
and finely sliced

150 g coconut meat, grated, steamed
for 3 minutes and cooled

4 Tbsp chopped lemon basil (*kemangi*)

2 Tbsp chopped fresh mint

4 Tbsp lime juice

1. Bring stock together with two-thirds of the spice blend, lemongrass and lime leaves to a boil. Add prawns and bring liquid back to a boil. Reduce heat and simmer prawns at very low heat until prawns are cooked, which will take only about 2 minutes. Retain the stock by scooping the prawns from the stock and plunging them into ice water for 30 seconds. Drain the water and peel the prawns.

2. Marinate squid with remaining spice blend and vacuum cook at 50°C for 10 minutes (see page 34).

3. Combine prawns and squid with all ingredients for the dressing, mixing well.

4. Season to taste with salt and ground white pepper.

5. Garnish as desired and serve.

NOTE
Be sure to use only the freshest squid, which must be washed and cleaned of any impurity. Slice the squid into 0.5-cm thick slivers rather than rings. Avoid cooking squid rapidly as this will immediately toughen the flesh and make it rubbery. Do not exceed temperatures over 50°C.

Noodle Salad *(Rujak Mie)* South Sumatra

fish fillet 600 g, skinned and
   cut into 1.5-cm cubes

1 pinch salt

$1/4$ tsp crushed white pepper

seafood spice blend (page 40)

1 litre light chicken stock (page 44)

oil for deep-frying

160 g tofu (page 163)

rice flour, as needed

2 Tbsp dried shrimps

160 g egg noodles

120 g glass noodles, soaked in hot water
   to soften, cut into 7-cm lengths

DRESSING

100 g shallots, peeled and sliced

40 g garlic, peeled and sliced

4 Tbsp rice vinegar

4 Tbsp sweet soy sauce (*kecap manis*)

1 Tbsp salty soy sauce (*kecap asin*)

salt, to taste

GARNISH

100 g cucumber, seeded and diced

100 g pineapple, peeled and diced

2 Tbsp fried shallots

50 g spring onions (scallions),
   finely sliced

50 g celery leaves, finely sliced

1. To prepare fish paste, season fish fillet with salt and pepper, then coat evenly with seafood spice blend.

2. To make the dumplings, warm stock to 80°C. Using two teaspoons, shape small oblong dumplings from basic fish paste and place into stock. Let cook for 5 minutes or until dumplings float to the surface. Drain and keep warm.

3. To prepare the dressing, combine shallots and garlic in a stone mortar or food processor and grind into a fine paste. Gradually add all other ingredients and grind into a smooth dressing. Set aside.

4. Heat oil for deep-frying over medium heat. Dust tofu with rice flour and deep-fry till crisp and golden. Drain on paper towels and cut into 1-cm cubes. Set aside.

5. Place dried shrimps in a stone mortar or food processor and process until fine.

6. Blanch egg noodles briefly in stock. Place into four large, deep soup plates. Repeat with glass noodles.

7. Garnish with cucumber, pineapple, fried shallots, sliced spring onions and celery leaves. Serve dressing on the side.

Prawn Salad with Tomatoes and Lemon Basil

(Peco Doang) South Sulawesi

1 kg medium-sized prawns with shells,
  cut off swimming legs and antennas

250 g cherry tomatoes, grilled for
  1 minute and peeled, cut into halves

4 Tbsp lemon basil (*kemangi*), sliced

4 Tbsp lime juice

salt, to taste

SPICE BLEND

60 g large red chillies, grilled until evenly
  brown, halved, seeded and sliced

4-7 bird's eye chillies, grilled and
  finely sliced

30 g candlenuts, roasted until golden

$1/4$ tsp salt

1. Grill or pan-fry prawns without oil for 1 minute. Allow to cool and peel shell. Reserve prawn shells for your next seafood stock.

2. Cut prawns into halves and then into even 1-cm cubes.

3. To make the spice blend, combine all ingredients in a stone mortar or food processor and grind into a fine paste.

4. Combine all ingredients and blend well. Season to taste with salt.

NOTE

This typical Bugis dish can also be prepared by adding three-quarters ripe mangoes, which adds a delicious note to this already very tasty prawn dish. Replace the tomatoes with mangoes or use tomatoes and mangoes together as they complement each other. In South Sumatra where prawns are expensive, this delicate shellfish is not sliced but ground roughly in a stone mortar. The dish serves more as a dressing than a salad and is eaten together with rice.

Marinated Tuna *(Gohu Ikan)* *Maluku*

This simple yet delicious tuna dish is never served chilled but consumed at room temperature. If you would like to serve this dish chilled then replace the coconut oil with good quality extra virgin olive oil. Coconut oil cannot be used for this dish as it will instantly solidify when chilled. In Ternate where this dish originates, low quality tuna is normally used and served with cassava bread, which can be replaced with a seafood cracker.

600 g tuna loin, cut into 0.5-cm cubes
3 Tbsp coconut oil
100 g shallots, very finely sliced
3-5 bird's eye chillies, finely sliced
3 Tbsp lime juice zest of 1 lime
3 Tbsp very finely sliced lemon basil (*kemangi*)
salt, to taste

1. Place tuna in a bowl.

2. In another bowl, combine all other ingredients, except salt, and mix well.

3. Drizzle dressing over tuna and mix well. Season to taste with salt.

Duck Salad with Green Papayas (*Lawar Kuwir*) *Bali*

When selecting green papayas make certain that you choose very green and firm fruits.
Remember that papayas, like pears, ripen from inside out which means that often the
skin appears still green while the flesh inside is already yellowish. If this is the case,
wrap the fruit in several layers of paper and allow the fruit to completely ripen.

400 g green papayas, peeled, halved, seeded and sliced into fine strips and blanched (Do not cool in ice water. After blanching, simply allow excess steam and water to evaporate.)

150 g grated coconut, lightly roasted

1 Tbsp finely grated palm sugar

2 Tbsp fried garlic

2 large red chillies, halved, seeded, finely sliced and fried until golden

2–3 bird's eye chillies, finely sliced and fried until golden (Adjust amount according to preference.)

2–3 kaffir lime leaves, finely chopped

salt and pepper, to taste

2 Tbsp fried shallots

DRESSING

2 Tbsp cooking oil

100 g spice blend for meat (page 40)

300 g minced duck meat, or giblets (heart, liver, stomach)

125 ml chicken or duck stock (page 44)

125 ml coconut cream

salt and pepper, to taste

2 Tbsp lime juice

1. To make the dressing, heat oil in a heavy saucepan, add spice blend and sauté until fragrant.

2. Season minced duck with salt and pepper and add to spice paste. Continue to sauté until meat changes colour.

3. Add stock and coconut cream, bring to a boil, then lower heat and simmer for 1 minute.

4. Season to taste with salt, pepper and lime juice. Cool to room temperature.

5. In a deep bowl combine all ingredients except the fried shallots and mix well with the dressing. Garnish with fried shallots.

Beef Salad with Lime and Mint *(Dojang Nuru)* *Flores*

Pork or chicken can be used in place of beef in this tasty recipe. The preparation process is the same, regardless of the type of meat used in the recipe. If using pork, choose a lean cut. If using chicken, slowly boil a whole chicken in chicken stock or use leftover roasted chicken that has been finely shredded.

60 ml vegetable or coconut oil

800 g beef topside, cut into four steaks and brined for 8 hours (see page 32)

150 g beef spice blend for meat

2 lemongrass, bruised

3 salam leaves

1 litre beef stock (page 44)

DRESSING

60 g shallots, peeled and finely sliced

2 large red chillies, halved, seeded and finely sliced

150 g coconut, roughly grated and steamed for 3 minutes and cooled

4 Tbsp roughly chopped lemon basil (*kemangi*)

2 Tbsp roughly chopped fresh mint

4 Tbsp lime juice

salt, to taste

ground white pepper, to taste

GARNISH

lime wedges

mint leaves

1. Heat 3 Tbsp oil in a frying pan and quickly sear beef steaks golden on each side.

2. In a pressure cooker pot, heat remaining oil. Add spice blend, lemongrass and salam leaves and sauté until fragrant.

3. Fill pot with hot beef stock and bring to a simmer. Remove scum as it accumulates.

4. Add beef and bring back to a simmer. Pressure cook at 1 bar / 15 psi for 45 minutes (see pages 21-22). Turn off heat and allow pot to cool for 30 minutes. Cool beef in stock to room temperature.

5. To check if beef is soft, tender and fully cooked, insert a *satay* skewer through to the centre of the meat. Use the skewer to lift the meat out of the stock. If the meat slides easily off the skewer, then the meat is done. The skewer should still be dry. If the meat is not yet fully cooked, it will not slide easily off the skewer and the skewer will look wet.

6. Cut meat into 1 x 0.5-cm cubes.

7. Combine meat with all ingredients for the dressing. Mix well.

8. Season to taste with salt and ground white pepper.

9. Garnish with fresh lime wedges and sprigs of fresh mint.

SOUPS

Green Papaya and Corn Soup with Seafood

(Gedang Mekuah) Bali

When preparing this dish, it is of utmost importance not to allow the soup to simmer once seafood is added. As with any other protein, take the fish out of refrigeration 1 hour before using and allow it to warm to room temperature. Once the soup is ready, add the seafood, give it a good gentle blend and adjust the final seasoning.

320 g assorted seafood of your choice (shrimps, scallops, fish, mussels etc), sliced

250 g seafood spice blend (page 40)

45 ml vegetable or coconut oil

2 stalks lemongrass, bruised

2 kaffir lime leaves, bruised

300 g green papaya, peeled, halved, seeded, and cut into ³/₄-cm cubes

1 litre seafood stock (page 46)

300 g corn kernels, steamed

250 ml coconut cream

salt, to taste

2 Tbsp lime juice

1 lime zest

2 Tbsp sliced spring onions (scallions), chopped celery leaves, chopped fresh lemon basil (*kemangi*)

1. Marinate seafood with 3 Tbsp seafood spice blend at room temperature for 1 hour.

2. Heat oil in saucepan, add remaining spice blend, lemongrass and kaffir lime leaves and sauté over medium heat for 2 minutes until fragrant.

3. Add papaya cubes and continue to sauté for 2 more minutes while continuously mixing.

4. Fill saucepan with stock, bring to a boil and simmer over low heat until papayas are 90% soft.

5. Add corn kernels and continue to simmer until the papayas are almost done.

6. Add coconut cream and bring back to a simmer. Season to taste with salt, lime juice and lime zest.

7. Just before serving, add seafood, blend well and garnish with spring onions, celery leaves and lemon basil.

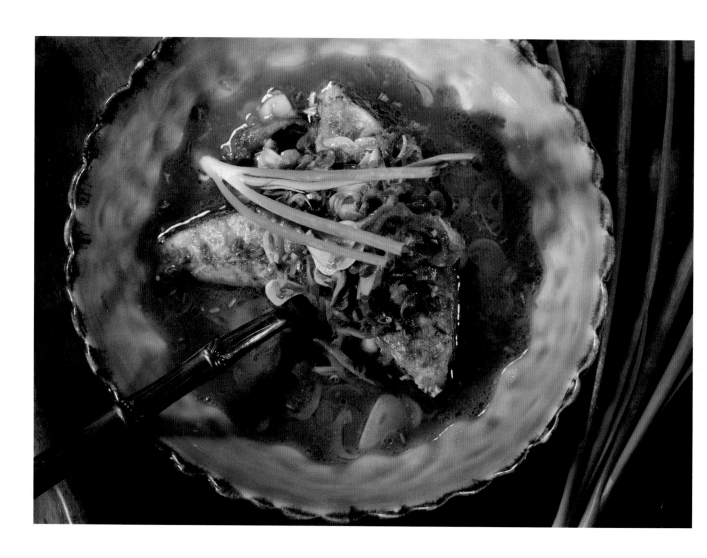

Fish Soup with Sour Mangoes *(Palu Cela)* South Sulawesi

1.2 kg whole fish, cleaned and
    sliced 2-cm thick

salt, to taste

2 Tbsp lime juice + more to taste

6 Tbsp coconut oil

75 g shallots, peeled and finely sliced

35 g garlic, peeled and finely sliced

30 g dried sour mangoes, washed
    and dried

800 ml seafood stock (page 46)

ground white pepper, to taste

a handful of finely sliced spring onions
    (scallions)

SPICE PASTE

60 g large red chillies, halved, seeded
    and sliced

3-5 bird's eye chillies, finely sliced

30 g turmeric, peeled and finely sliced

1. To make the spice paste, combine chillies and turmeric in a stone mortar or food processor and grind into a fine paste. Reserve one-third of the spice paste to marinate the fillets.

2. Season sliced fish with salt and lime juice and rub evenly with one-third of the spice blend. Heat 3 Tbsp vegetable oil in a saucepan and quickly sear fish slices (10 seconds on each side). Vacuum cook (see page 34).

3. Heat 3 Tbsp oil in a soup pan. Add sliced shallots and garlic and sauté for 2 minutes over medium heat.

4. Add remaining ground spices and continue to sauté until fragrant. Add sour mangoes and sauté again for 1 more minute.

5. Fill up with stock and bring to simmer for 5 minutes. Season to taste with salt, white pepper and lime juice.

6. Arrange fish fillets in soup bowl and fill up with soup. Garnish with sliced spring onions.

NOTE

This is home cooking at its very best and great for the weight conscious. Not much is involved in preparing this delicious and very light dish. All one needs to do is to get the freshest fish possible and to be extra careful when poaching the fish. Although the fish can be cooked simply in a stock, it is a lot juicier and tastier if the fish is sealed in a plastic bag and then poached in a temperature-controlled water bath. Keep temperature as low as possible.

Freshwater Fish Soup *(Pindang Palembang)* South Sumatra

2 stalks lemongrass, bruised

2 salam leaves

2 large red chillies, sliced

6-8 bird's eye chillies

800 ml light seafood or chicken stock (page 46 or 44)

2 Tbsp sweet soy sauce (*kecap manis*)

4 Tbsp tamarind water (see page 69)

1.2 kg freshwater fish, head removed, cleaned and cut into 4 even slices, brined for 5 hours (see page 32)

120 g tomatoes, peeled, halved, seeded and sliced. Strain seeds and keep liquid for soup

2 Tbsp finely sliced spring onions (scallions)

2 Tbsp lemon basil (*kemangi*), roughly chopped

2 Tbsp lime juice

salt, to taste

SPICE BLEND

2 Tbsp coconut oil

30 g shallots, peeled and sliced

20 g garlic, peeled and sliced

50 g large red chillies, halved, seeded and sliced

20 g galangal (*laos*), peeled and sliced

20 g ginger, peeled and sliced

1. To make the spice blend, combine all ingredients in a stone mortar or food processor and grind into a fine paste.

2. Transfer ground spices into a saucepan, add lemongrass and salam leaves and sauté over medium heat until fragrant. Reserve one-third of the spice blend and cool.

3. Add sliced chillies and continue to sauté for 2 more minutes. Fill up with stock, add soy sauce and tamarind water and bring to a boil. Simmer for 5 minutes.

4. Drain brine from fish fillets.

5. Marinate fish fillets with the reserved one-third spice paste and vacuum pack. Allow to rest for 1 hour in refrigerator.

6. Vacuum cook fish at 50°C (see page 34). Fillets 2.5-cm thick will take about 25 minutes to reach their target temperature. Thinner pieces may need just 15 minutes.

7. To complete the soup, add tomatoes, spring onions and lemon basil and simmer for 1 more minute. Season to taste with lime juice and salt.

Fried Fish Simmered in Spiced Court Bouillon

(Ikan Cuka) West Sumatra

800 g fish fillet of your choice (tuna, mackerel, mahi mahi, snapper or portion-sized whole mackerels)

60 ml coconut oil for frying

MARINADE

75 g ginger

75 g galangal (*laos*)

75 g garlic

2 Tbsp rice vinegar (optional lime juice)

DRESSING

2 Tbsp coconut oil

200 g shallots, peeled

100 g small garlic, peeled

75 g large red chillies, whole

75 g large green chillies

3 salam leaves

3 kaffir lime leaves

1 turmeric leaf, torn

600 ml seafood stock (page 46)

75 ml rice vinegar

salt, to taste

ground white pepper, to taste

1. Brine fish for 3–5 hours as described on page 32. Rinse fillets under running tap water and pat dry.

2. To make the marinade, combine all ingredients in a stone mortar or food processor and grind into a very fine paste. Reserve half of the marinade for the dressing.

3. Marinate fish with half of the marinade and refrigerate for 1 hour or vacuum pack for a better result.

4. Heat oil in a shallow frying pan and very quickly fry fish on both sides until a little golden.

5. To prepare the dressing, heat oil in a saucepan. Add the reserved half of the marinade and quickly fry for 1 minute until fragrant. Add shallots, garlic, chillies and leaves and sauté over medium heat for 2 minutes. Fill saucepan with seafood stock and rice vinegar and simmer over medium heat for 7 minutes. Season to taste with salt and white pepper.

6. Vacuum cook fish at 45°C (see page 34). Fillets that are 1.5-cm thick will take about 15 minutes. Thicker pieces and whole fish will take a little longer.

7. Combine fish fillets and soup.

Sour Hot Seafood Soup *(Kuah Asam Pedas) Maluku*

This soup is Maluku's version of the French bouillabaisse with a noticeable
Portuguese influence. This is a dish that is full of flavour and delectable soft textures.
The people of Maluku mostly use sardines or cheap mackerels for this fish soup.

SPICE PASTE

3 Tbsp coconut oil

50 g shallots, peeled and sliced

30 g garlic, peeled and sliced

75 g large red chillies, halved, seeded
and sliced

5-7 bird's eye chillies, finely sliced

30 g turmeric, peeled, sliced and
finely chopped

30 g ginger, peeled, sliced and finely
chopped

50 g peanuts without skin, lightly roasted

¹/₄ tsp crushed white peppercorns

2 lemongrass, bruised

4 kaffir lime leaves, bruised

1 litre seafood or chicken stock
(page 46 or 44)

3 Tbsp tamarind water (see page 69)

200 g tomatoes, grilled, peeled, seeded
and diced (keep the juice)

3 Tbsp lime juice

salt, to taste

800 g-1 kg assorted seafood or only
one type, cleaned

3 Tbsp finely sliced lemon basil (*kemangi*)

1. To make the spice paste, combine all ingredients in a stone
   mortar or food processor and grind into a fine paste.

2. Transfer ground spice paste into a soup kettle, add
   lemongrass and kaffir lime leaves and sauté for 2 minutes
   until fragrant. Reserve one-third of the spice paste and cool.

3. Fill kettle with stock, tamarind juice and tomatoes and bring
   to a boil. Simmer over low heat for 5 minutes. Season to taste
   with lime juice and salt.

4. Combine seafood and reserved spice blend and mix well.
   Vacuum cook seafood to a core temperature of 45°C (see
   page 34) , which will take 25 minutes.

5. Combine stock, seafood and tomatoes and cook at 45°C for
   5 minutes.

6. Garnish with sliced lemon basil.

Seafood Soup *(Sop Ikan)* Bali

1 Tbsp coconut or vegetable oil

$^1/_2$ cup seafood spice paste (page 40)

1 stalk lemongrass, bruised

2 lime leaves, torn

2 sour starfruits (*blimbing buluh*) (optional)

3 small bird's eye chillies, to taste

$^2/_3$ cup seafood stock (page 46)

100 g tomatoes, peeled, halved, seeded and sliced

100 g cucumbers, halved, seeded, sliced and blanched for 30 seconds

600 g assorted seafood (fish fillet, prawn, squid, crab, mussels, scallops etc.), cleaned

1 Tbsp lime juice + more to taste

1 pinch salt + more to taste

pepper, to taste

zest of $^1/_2$ lime

1 Tbsp finely sliced spring onions (scallions)

1 Tbsp finely chopped lemon basil

1. Heat oil in heavy saucepan. Add half of the spice paste, lemongrass, lime leaves, starfruits and small chillies and sauté over medium heat for two minutes or until fragrant.

2. Add seafood stock and bring to a very light simmer for 5 minutes. Add tomatoes and cucumbers.

3. Marinate seafood with remaining seafood spice paste, lime juice and salt. Blend well.

4. Place seafood into a heatproof plastic bag and seal.

5. Vacuum cook at 50°C for 15 minutes (see page 34).

6. Open bags and pour the juice from the seafood into the simmering stock. Blend well and season to taste with salt, pepper, lime juice and lime zest.

7. Arrange seafood in serving dish and cover with soup.

8. Garnish with sliced spring onions and chopped lemon basil.

Sour starfruit *Blimbing buluh*

This small fruit is of the same species as the better-known starfruit, but it is extremely sour and is used almost entirely as a flavouring. It is occasionally called sour finger carambola. If not available replace with segments of lime.

Prawn Noodle Soup *(Tek Wan)* South Sumatra

600 g fish fillet, skinned and cut into
 1.5-cm cubes

125 g seafood spice blend (page 40)

1 pinch salt

$1/4$ tsp crushed white pepper

1.5 litres seafood or chicken stock
 (page 46 or 44)

200 g medium-sized prawns (shrimp),
 peeled, deveined and halved

120 g glass noodles, cooked

50 g dry wood ear mushrooms, soaked
 in warm water for 15 minutes

4 Tbsp finely sliced spring onions
 (scallions)

4 Tbsp fried shallots

SAUCE

5 Tbsp rice vinegar

5 Tbsp sweet soy sauce (*kecap manis*)

5 Tbsp salty soy sauce (*kecap asin*)

salt, to taste

(*This page, left*)

1. To make fish paste, season fish fillet with salt and pepper, then coat evenly with seafood spice blend.

2. Make fish dumplings using two teaspoons to shape fish paste into oblongs.

3. Bring stock to a simmer and poach dumplings at 80°C for 5 minutes or until they float to the surface. Place dumplings in serving bowls and set aside.

4. Place prawns into a soup strainer and cook for 1 minute in simmering stock. Place into serving bowls with dumplings.

5. Heat noodles briefly in stock. Divide among prepared serving bowls.

6. Cut wood ear mushrooms into even pieces and poach in stock for 1 minute. Ladle soup with wood ear mushrooms into serving bowls over noodles.

7. Garnish with sliced spring onions and fried shallots.

8. Combine all ingredients for sauce and serve on the side with noodle soup.

Prawn Noodle Soup with Coconut

(Celimpungan) *South Sumatra*

This delicious creamy seafood soup is virtually identical to *tek wan*; the only additional ingredient is coconut milk.

600 g fish fillet, skinned and cut into 1.5-cm cubes

125 g seafood spice blend (page 40)

1 pinch salt

1/4 tsp crushed white pepper

1 litre seafood or chicken stock (page 46 or 44)

500 ml coconut milk

200 g medium-sized prawns (shrimp), peeled, deveined and halved

120 g glass noodles, cooked

50 g dry wood ear mushrooms, soaked in warm water for 15 minutes

2 Tbsp finely sliced spring onions (scallions)

2 Tbsp fried shallots

SAUCE

1 Tbsp rice vinegar

1 Tbsp sweet soy sauce (*kecap manis*)

1 Tbsp salty soy sauce (*kecap asin*)

salt, to taste

(*Refer to page 90, right*)

1. To prepare fish paste, season fish fillet with salt and pepper, then coat evenly with seafood spice blend.

2. Make fish dumplings using two teaspoons to shape fish paste into oblongs.

3. Bring stock and coconut milk to a simmer. Poach dumplings at 80°C for 5 minutes or until they float to the surface. Place dumplings in serving bowls and set aside.

4. Place prawns into a soup strainer and cook for 1 minute in simmering broth. Place into serving bowls with dumplings.

5. Heat noodles briefly in stock. Divide among prepared serving bowls.

6. Cut wood ear mushrooms into even pieces and poach in stock for 1 minute. Ladle soup with wood ear mushrooms into serving bowls over noodles.

7. Divide all ingredients evenly into four large soup bowls and fill up with soup.

8. Garnish with sliced spring onions and fried shallots.

9. Combine all ingredients for sauce and serve on the side with noodle soup.

Beef Soup (*Coto Makasar*) South Sulawesi

4 litres beef stock (page 44)

3 Tbsp oil for frying

500 g beef shoulder or brisket

500 g ox tongue

500 g beef tripe, thoroughly washed and cut into 3 x 10-cm stripes

salt, to taste

lime juice, to taste

a handful of sliced spring onions

2 Tbsp fried shallots

SPICE PASTE

2 Tbsp coconut oil

60 g shallots, peeled and sliced

30 g garlic, peeled and sliced

30 g galangal (*laos*), peeled and finely sliced

30 g ginger, peeled and finely sliced

3-6 bird's eye chillies, sliced (adjust amount according to preference)

20 g candlenuts, crushed

60 g raw peanuts without skin, crushed

1 Tbsp coriander seeds, roasted

1 Tbsp caraway seeds

¼ tsp crushed white pepper

2 stalks lemongrass, bruised

4 lime leaves, bruised

2 salam leaves

(*Refer to page 93, left*)

1. To make the spice paste, combine all ingredients except lemongrass, lime leaves and salam leaves in a stone mortar or food processor and grind into a very fine paste. Place ground ingredients into a pressure cooker, add remaining ingredients and sauté over medium heat until spices are fragrant.

2. Fill the cooker with beef stock and bring to a boil. (In traditional South Sulawesi cuisine, cooks would use the water in which the rice had been soaked for 20 minutes prior to cooking.)

3. Heat 3 Tbsp oil in a frying pan and quickly brown the beef shoulder evenly on each side. This will add a meatier flavour to the broth.

4. Place all meats into the beef soup, bring back to a boil and skim off scum.

5. Pressure cook at a gauge pressure of 1 bar / 15 psi for 45 minutes (see pages 21-22). Start timing when full pressure is reached. Let the cooker cool for 20–30 minutes.

6. Remove the cover, take out the ox tongue and plunge into ice water. Peel off skin.

7. Cut each cut of meat into small bite-sized pieces and warm in beef soup before serving.

8. Season beef soup to taste with salt and a generous squeeze of lime juice. Garnish with sliced spring onions and fried shallots.

NOTE

Serve with rice cakes or steamed rice and fermented tomato soybean sauce.

Beef Soup with Glass Noodles and Potato Patties

(Sup Sodara) South Sulawesi

The preparation is in many ways very similar to *coto makassar* on page 92. As *sup sodara* does not include any beef intestines, the dish would definitely appeal to Western cooks. To garnish the soup, add glass noodles and pan-fried potato cakes. Sprinkle with fried shallots and sliced spring onions.

PAN-FRIED POTATO PATTIES

500 g potatoes (skin on), boiled or steamed in salt water

2 Tbsp fried shallots

50 g celery stalks, finely sliced

1 egg yolk

1 pinch salt

1 pinch ground white pepper

1 egg, beaten

vegetable oil, for frying

glass noodles, soaked in warm water for 15 minutes

(This page, right)

1. Peel potatoes when still warm. Grate roughly when cold with Roesti grater.

2. Combine potatoes, fried shallots, celery stalks, egg yolk, salt and pepper, then blend well.

3. Form small patties and turn in beaten egg.

4. Pan-fry in vegetable oil until patties are golden on both sides.

Beef Rib Soup *(Pindang Palembang)* *South Sumatra*

2 stalks lemongrass, bruised

2 salam leaves

1.6 kg beef ribs, cut into 100 g portions

2 litres beef or chicken stock (page 44)

3 large green chillies

6-8 bird's eye chillies

80 g onion, peeled, halved and finely sliced

2 Tbsp sweet soy sauce (*kecap manis*)

2 Tbsp salty soy sauce (*kecap asin*)

4 Tbsp tamarind water (see page 69)

salt, to taste

120 g tomatoes, peeled, halved, seeded and sliced

2 Tbsp roughly sliced lemon basil (*kemangi*)

2 Tbsp finely sliced spring onions (scallions)

SPICE PASTE

2 Tbsp coconut oil

30 g shallots, peeled and sliced

20 g garlic, peeled and sliced

50 g large red chillies, halved, seeded and sliced

20 g galangal (*laos*), peeled and sliced

20 g turmeric, peeled and sliced

20 g ginger, peeled and sliced

1. To make the spice paste, combine all ingredients in a stone mortar or food processor and grind into a fine paste.

2. Transfer ground spices into a pressure cooker, add lemongrass and salam leaves and sauté over medium heat until fragrant. Add beef ribs and continue to sauté for 5 minutes over medium heat until ribs are evenly coated and change colour. Add three-quarters of the stock, chillies and onion. Mix well and bring to a boil. Skim off scum and cover with pressure cooker cover.

3. Pressure cook at a gauge pressure of 1 bar /15 psi for 45 minutes (see pages 21-22). Start timing when full pressure is reached. Let the cooker cool for 20 minutes.

4. Open cover and check if meat is cooked; if necessary, continue to simmer over very low heat until meat is so soft that it almost falls off the bones.

5. Season soup with soy sauce, tamarind water and salt to taste. Just before serving, add tomato slices, lemon basil and sliced spring onions. Mix well.

Palembang

Palembang is the capital city of South Sumatra and one of the oldest cities in Indonesia, with a history of being the capital of a maritime empire. Located on the banks of the Muri River on the east coast of southern Sumatra, Palembang has an area of 400.61 sq km and a population of almost 1,500,000. It is Sumatra's second-largest city after Medan and the seventh-largest city in Indonesia. No visit to this vibrant busy city would be complete without eating *pindang*, a richly flavoured meat or fish soup.

Beef Soup with Potatoes and Eggs

(Soto Padang) *West Sumatra*

Soto padang is the Indonesian version of a French Pot-au-Feu. In Padang, this hearty
soup is served as breakfast. It is irresistible when served together with creamed egg tea
(page 195)

2 kg beef bones, chopped into
walnut-sized pieces

3 salam leaves

3 kaffir lime leaf, bruised

2 stalks lemongrass, bruised

2 litres beef stock (page 44)

1 litre water

600 g beef brisket, thoroughly washed,
drained and dried, cut into
3 x 200 g pieces

200 g glass noodles, soaked in warm
water for 15 minutes

4 Tbsp finely-sliced spring onions
(scallions)

2 Tbsp finely sliced celery leaves

2 Tbsp fried shallots

1 poached chicken egg

POTATO PATTIES

600 g small potatoes with skin

1 pinch nutmeg, ground

2 Tbsp finely chopped celery leaves

3 Tbsp finely sliced spring onions
(scallions)

salt, to taste

ground white pepper, to taste

3 Tbsp rice flour

2 eggs, beaten

SPICE PASTE

3 Tbsp coconut oil

50 g shallots, peeled and finely sliced

25 g garlic, peeled and finely sliced

30 g turmeric, peeled and finely sliced

40 g ginger, peeled and finely sliced

30 g galangal (*laos*), peeled and
finely sliced

1/2 tsp finely crushed cardamom

1/4 tsp finely crushed white peppercorns

1. Rinse bones until water is clear, place in a stockpot and
cover with cold water and bring to a boil over high heat.
Drain and discard water. Wash bones again under
running water.

2. To make the spice paste, combine all ingredients in a stone
mortar or food processor and grind into a very fine paste.
Transfer spice paste into a pressure cooker pot, add salam
and kaffir lime leaves, lemongrass and sauté until fragrant.

3. Add rinsed bones, fill cooker with beef stock and 1 litre of
water and bring to a boil. Remove scum as it accumulates.
Add beef briskets, cover cooker with pressure cover and
pressure cook at a gauge pressure of 1 bar /15 psi for
1 hour (see pages 21-22). Start timing when full pressure
is reached.

4. Let the cooker cool for 20 minutes.

5. Lift the meat from the cooking liquid with a slotted spoon,
and transfer to another pan. Cover with 2 cups of stock and
allow meat to cool to room temperature.

6. Strain remaining stock, which will be the main base for
your soup.

7. To make the potato patties, place potatoes into a small pot,
and fill it with cold salted water. Bring to a boil and simmer
uncovered until potatoes are 90% cooked. To check if
potatoes are cooked, push a bamboo skewer into the centre
of the potato. The skewer must be dry when retracted. Drain
the water and allow steam to evaporate and potatoes to
cool. Peel potatoes and grate roughly with a Roesti grater.
Combine grated potatoes with nutmeg, celery and spring
onions and season to taste with salt and ground white
pepper. Shape into small patties. Dust with rice flour and
turn in beaten egg.

8. Heat 3 Tbsp vegetable oil in a non-stick pan, add patties and fry over medium heat until golden and crispy.

9. To serve the soup, bring beef stock to a simmer and season to taste with salt. Heat glass noodles for 20 seconds in simmering broth and transfer into individual soup bowls. Slice beef evenly and arrange into each bowl. Top with one poached chicken egg and fill with beef soup. Garnish with potato patties and some finely sliced spring onions. Complete the soup with finely sliced celery leaves and fried shallots.

FISH & SEAFOOD

Prawns in Spiced Tomato Sauce

(Udang Saus Padang) West Sumatra

Fresh tender squid prepared in the same way will also work well for this recipe. Served at room temperature, these spicy prawns make a terrific appetizer. They can be served with crispy crackers or steamed rice cakes (page 173).

150 g large red chillies, halved, seeded and sliced

5-7 bird's eye chillies, finely sliced

75 g shallots, peeled and sliced

20 g garlic, peeled and sliced

600 g prawns (shrimps), peeled and cleaned

2 Tbsp lime juice + more to taste

3 Tbsp coconut oil

20 g ginger, peeled, sliced and bruised

1 salam leaf

2 kaffir lime leaves, torn

60 g onions, peeled and finely sliced

30 g leek, finely sliced

150 g tomato, grilled, peeled, seeded and diced (keep liquid)

1 Tbsp red tomato anchovy sauce (page 62)

1 Tbsp oyster sauce

250 ml seafood stock (page 46)

salt, to taste

1. Combine chillies, shallots and garlic in a stone mortar or food processor and grind into a very fine paste.

2. Marinate prawns with 2 Tbsp chilli-garlic-shallot paste, and 2 Tbsp lime juice.

3. Heat coconut oil in a saucepan. Add remaining ground paste, ginger, salam and lime leaves and sauté for 1 minute until fragrant. Add onions and leek and continue to sauté over medium heat for 2 more minutes.

4. Add tomatoes, red anchovy tomato sauce and oyster sauce. Mix well and sauté for 2 more minutes.

5. Add stock and bring back to a simmer.

6. Add prawns, mix well and simmer over low heat for 2 minutes.

7. *Optional: vacuum cook prawns or cook in ziplock bag (see page 34).*

8. Season to taste with salt and lime juice.

Sweet and Sour Fried Prawns (*Udang Krupuk*) *West Sumatra*

Every night, just before sundown along the shore of Padang, vendors set up their small food stalls to sell this very popular and tasty snack. Deep-fried in advance, they are displayed in small street kitchens to hungry customers. The prawns are crispy and the sweet, sour spicy chilli sauce extremely addictive.

75 g large red chillies, halved, seeded and sliced

3-5 bird's eye chillies, finely sliced

30 g shallots, peeled and sliced

20 g garlic, peeled and sliced

600 g prawns (shrimps), peeled and cleaned. In Padang very small prawns that are not shelled or deveined are used.

50 g rice flour

300 ml frying batter (page 29)

oil for frying

SAUCE

150 g large red chillies, halved, seeded and sliced

3-5 bird's eye chillies, finely sliced

20 g garlic, peeled and finely sliced

75 g shallots, peeled and sliced

70 g tomatoes, grilled, peeled and diced

30 g white sugar

30 ml rice vinegar

45 ml tomato juice

salt, to taste

1 Tbsp lime juice

1. Combine chillies, shallots and garlic in a stone mortar or food processor and grind into a very fine paste. Add prawns and mix well.

2. Dust prawns evenly with rice flour and dip one by one into the frying batter.

3. Deep-fry until golden (see page 29).

4. To make the sauce, combine chillies, garlic and shallots in a stone mortar or food processor and grind into a very fine paste. Transfer to a saucepan.

5. Add diced tomatoes, sugar, vinegar and tomato juice and simmer for 5 minutes over low heat until the sauce is fragrant and lightly creamy. Season to taste with salt and 1 Tbsp of lime juice.

6. Blend sauce using an immersion blender, or a counter top blender for larger quantities.

Coconut Prawns in Banana Leaf *(Palem Udang)* *Bali*

This is the perfect dish for dinner parties and barbecues as it can be prepared in advance. Make certain to thaw it for at least 1 hour before cooking and warm to room temperature. The safest way to ensure that the dish is perfectly cooked is to insert a probe into the centre of the banana-leaf-wrapped parcel and allow it to steam until a core temperature of 50°C is reached.

600 g prawns (shrimps) without shell, cleaned, deveined and cut into 1-cm cubes

120 g seafood spice blend (page 40)

120 g freshly grated coconut

120 ml coconut cream

3 Tbsp fried shallots

1 Tbsp fried garlic

2-4 bird's eye chillies, finely chopped (adjust amount according to preference)

2 Tbsp lime juice

salt, to taste

black pepper, to taste

4 kaffir lime leaves, bruised

2 Tbsp finely sliced lemon basil (*kemangi*)

8 banana leaf wrappers, 20 x 25-cm each

2 medium-sized tomatoes, sliced

1. Combine prawns, seafood spice blend, grated coconut, coconut cream, shallots, garlic, bird's eye chillies and lime juice in a large bowl and blend well. Season to taste with salt and black pepper.

2. Soften each banana leaf wrapper by holding it over a gas flame or soaking it in boiling water or microwaving it for 3 seconds.

3. Place kaffir lime leaves and one-quarter of the sliced basil in the centre of a banana leaf wrapper. Top with one-quarter of the prawn mix and cover with a few slices of tomatoes.

4. Take one long edge of the wrapper and fold it towards the centre to cover the ingredients, then roll up tightly. Secure open ends with bamboo skewer.

5. Steam parcels for 5 minutes to a core temperature of 50°C, then charcoal grill for 2 minutes. Turn parcels over at least once.

Prawn Satay *(Satay Udang)* *Bali*

800 g prawn (shrimps) shelled, cleaned and brined for 1 hour (see page 32)

200 g seafood spice blend (page 40)

3-5 bird's eye chillies, finely chopped

15 g palm sugar, finely grated

salt, to taste

75 ml vegetable or coconut oil

1. Combine prawns, 125 g seafood spice blend, bird's eye chillies, palm sugar and salt and mix well. Skewer 3 prawns tightly onto wooden satay skewers.

2. Combine 75 g seafood spice blend and 75 ml vegetable or coconut oil and mix well. Use as a basting mix.

3. Grill *satays* over very hot charcoal until golden brown, while frequently basting.

NOTE FOR SERVING

This tasty crunchy snack tastes even better when served with rice cakes (page 173) and a rich creamy peanut sauce (page 56). If you wish to prepare *satays* using pork, beef or chicken, follow the same directions for prawn *satay*, but replace with the respective spice blend. Use neck or tenderloin for pork, end cuts of tenderloins, sirloins or topside for beef and skinned and boneless legs for chicken. Make certain that the charcoal is extremely hot. The best *satays* are usually not just grilled but seared over glowing hot charcoal.

Prawn and Egg Ragout in Coconut Sauce

(Gulai Kentang Telor) West Sumatra

For this recipe, you can be flexible with the selection of ingredients as long as you follow the preparation method, which guarantees a tasty end result.

3 Tbsp vegetable or coconut oil

1 turmeric leaf

1 stalk lemongrass, bruised

125 ml coconut cream

375 ml vegetable stock (page 47)

600 g small potatoes, peeled, halved, rinsed and half-boiled in salt water

20 quail eggs, hard-boiled and peeled

200 g prawns (shrimps), peeled and cleaned

100 g petai, cleaned and blanched

salt, to taste

ground white pepper, to taste

spring onions (scallions), finely sliced, for garnishing

SPICE PASTE

50 g shallots, peeled and sliced

40 g garlic, peeled and sliced

100 g large red chillies, halved, seeded and sliced

30 g galangal (*laos*), peeled and sliced

30 g turmeric, peeled and sliced

30 g ginger, peeled and sliced

1. To make the spice paste, combine all ingredients in a stone mortar or food processor and grind into a fine paste.

2. Prepare coconut sauce. Heat oil in a heavy saucepan. Add spice paste, turmeric leaf and lemongrass and sauté until fragrant. Add coconut cream and vegetable stock and bring to a boil.

3. Add drained potatoes and bring back to a boil. Reduce heat and simmer over low heat until potatoes are 75% cooked.

4. Add eggs and continue to simmer until potatoes are almost soft. Add shrimps and petai and simmer for 2 more minutes.

5. Strain and transfer most of the coconut sauce sauce into a food processor and blend at high speed for 15 seconds.

6. Combine ingredients and sauce and season to taste with salt and ground white pepper. Garnish with sliced spring onions.

Prawn Noodles with Egg in Cream Sauce
(Mie Celor) South Sumatra

This is a popular breakfast dish in Palembang and is found all over the city. In roadside food stalls, all ingredients are pre-prepared and it takes the noodle vendor only a few seconds to prepare this delicious noodle dish. Pasta carbonara, the Indonesian way.

1 litre seafood stock (page 46)

400 g medium-sized prawns (shrimps), soaked in salted ice water for 2 hours, drained

2 litres water

200 g egg noodles, cooked and cooled

160 g bean sprouts, cleaned

4 chicken eggs or 14 quail eggs, hard-boiled or poached

2 Tbsp fried shallots

2 Tbsp finely sliced spring onions (scallions)

SAUCE

2 Tbsp coconut or vegetable oil

40 g shallots, peeled and finely sliced

20 g garlic, peeled and finely sliced

40 g large green or red chillies, halved, seeded and sliced

3-5 bird's eye chillies, sliced

1/2 Tbsp tapioca flour

400 ml seafood stock (page 46), cooled. (use the same stock in which you boiled the prawns)

100 ml coconut cream

salt, to taste

ground white pepper, to taste

1. Bring seafood stock to a boil. Add prawns and bring back to a boil. Simmer for 1 minute

2. Remove prawns from stock and plunge into ice water for 10 seconds. Drain ice water and peel prawns, cutting them lengthwise into halves.

3. Add prawn shells to stock and simmer over low heat for 30 minutes. Strain stock and discard shells.

4. To prepare the sauce, combine oil, shallots, garlic and chillies in a stone mortar or food processor and grind into a very fine paste. Transfer to a saucepan.

5. Sauté spice paste over medium heat until fragrant. Add flour and whisk well to ensure that there are no lumps. While continuously whisking, gradually add 400 ml of the cooled stock and bring sauce to a boil. This will take a few minutes and a little work as it is important to not stop whisking in order to prevent the sauce from sticking to the bottom of the pan. Once the sauce comes to a boil, add coconut cream, reduce heat and simmer sauce while whisking continuously. Season to taste with salt and ground white pepper.

6. In a separate pot, bring 2 litres of water to a boil. Heat noodles and beansprouts separately in a Chinese soup strainer and divide into four soup plates. Top with halved prawns and pour half cup sauce over.

7. Top with egg and garnish with fried shallots and spring onions.

Smoked Fish Cakes *(Kueh Cara)* Maluku

These little cakes make the perfect afternoon snack. In Maluku, smoked mackerel, sardine or bonito is used. Any smoked fish would work well as an alternative.

BATTER

180 g white wheat flour
445 g coconut milk
145 g coconut cream
185 g eggs
3 Tbsp coconut oil
1 lime, grated for zest
1 pinch nutmeg, finely grated
1 pinch salt

FILLING

1 Tbsp coconut oil
40 g shallots, peeled and finely sliced
20 g garlic, peeled and finely chopped
50 g almonds, roughly chopped
100 g smoked fish, finely shredded
  (use the finest you can find)
2 Tbsp finely sliced spring onions
  (scallions)
2 Tbsp finely sliced bird's eye chillies
2 Tbsp sliced celery leaves

1. Prepare batter. Combine flour, coconut milk and cream and mix well. Add eggs and stir together. Sieve mixture through a fine sieve. Add coconut oil, lime zest and grated nutmeg. Season to taste with a pinch of salt. Mix well. Allow mixture to rest for 30 minutes.

2. To make the filling, heat oil in a frying pan. Add shallots and garlic and sauté until lightly golden. Add almonds and mix well. Cool mixture. Combine mixture with smoked fish and spring onions.

3. Oil muffin pan and heat until very hot. Fill muffin cups half-full with batter. Top with $^{1}/_{2}$ Tbsp filling, sliced chillies and celery leaves.

4. Bake at 180°C for 7 minutes, then unmould cakes and place bottom-up on a pan to bake for another 3 minutes. Serve.

Smoked Fish in Coconut Dressing

(Bale Santang) South Sulawesi

This is a typical Bugis dish found in South Sulawesi. It is recommended that you smoke your own fish (see page 33) as you can adjust the taste and flavour of the dish.

800 g smoked fish, sliced into 60 g portions (to smoke your fish of choice see page 33)

375 ml seafood or chicken stock (page 46 or 44)

125 ml coconut cream

2 stalks lemongrass, bruised

salt, to taste

2 tsp lime juice + lime zest

cherry tomatoes, as desired, grilled, peeled and halved

sliced lemon basil (*kemangi*)

SPICE PASTE

75 g shallots, peeled and sliced

30 g garlic, peeled and sliced

10 g turmeric, peeled and sliced

30 g ginger, peeled and sliced

40 g large red chillies, halved, seeded and sliced

3-5 bird's eye chillies, sliced

1. Vacuum seal smoked fish and heat to 50°C for 15 minutes.

2. To make the spice paste, combine all ingredients in a stone mortar or food processor and grind into a very fine paste.

3. Combine stock, coconut cream, lemongrass and spice paste in a saucepan and simmer for 5 minutes over very low heat. Blend sauce with a hand blender for 30 seconds.

4. Season to taste with a pinch of salt, a generous squeeze of lime juice and some lime zest. Garnish with grilled tomatoes and lemon basil.

Spicy Fried River Fish *(Ikan Bumbu Acar)* South Sumatra

1.2 kg small river fish (optional sardines), cleaned, scaled and washed

1 pinch salt

1 pinch black peppercorns, crushed

3 Tbsp lime juice

50 g rice flour

oil for frying fish

a handful of lemon basil

DRESSING

3 Tbsp coconut oil

50 g large red chillies, halved, seeded and sliced

6-10 bird's eye chillies, finely sliced

30 g garlic, peeled and sliced

50 g shallots, peeled and sliced

30 g ginger, peeled and finely sliced

30 g galangal (*laos*), peeled and finely sliced

1 Tbsp palm sugar

2 Tbsp tamarind water (see page 69)

2 kaffir lime leaves, bruised

2 large tomatoes, peeled and cut into wedges

1/4 cup seafood or chicken stock (page 46 or 44)

1. Season fish with salt, pepper and lime juice. Dust evenly with rice flour.

2. Prepare dressing. Heat 3 Tbsp oil in a saucepan. Add chillies, garlic, shallots, ginger and galangal and sauté over medium heat for 3 minutes until fragrant. Add palm sugar, tamarind juice and kaffir lime leaves and continue to sauté for 2 more minutes. Add tomatoes and stock, then bring to simmer. Season to taste with salt, pepper and lime juice.

3. In a separate pan, heat frying oil to 160°C. Add fish and fry until golden. Drain on paper towels. Combine fish with tomato spice, then blend and stir well.

4. Garnish with fresh lemon basil and serve with lots of fresh greens such as cucumbers, green beans, winged beans, and sliced cabbage.

Smoked Fish Steamed in Banana Leaves
(Boboto) *Maluku*

Instead of using minced fish, cut fish fillets into 1.5-cm cubes and smoked fish into even strips. To further enhance the flavour, add one bruised kaffir lime leaf and some lemon basil to the banana leaf parcels.

400 g white fish fillet, cut into 1.5-cm cubes
200 g smoked fish, cut into strips
2 eggs, squashed
2 Tbsp tamarind water (see page 69)
2 Tbsp lime juice
salt, to taste
2 medium-sized tomatoes, finely sliced
sprigs of lemon basil (*kemangi*), as needed

SPICE BLEND
2 Tbsp coconut oil
40 g shallots, peeled and sliced
20 g garlic, peeled and sliced
30 g ginger, peeled and finely sliced
20 g turmeric, peeled and finely sliced
50 g peanuts without skin, lightly roasted

1. To prepare the spice paste, heat coconut oil in a frying pan. Add shallots, garlic, ginger and turmeric and sauté over medium heat for 2 minutes or until fragrant. Add peanuts and continue to sauté for 1 more minute. Set aside to cool before placing into a stone mortar or food processor and grinding into a fine paste.

2. Combine spice paste, fish, eggs, tamarind water and lime juice and season to taste with salt. Place a heaped tablespoon of the seafood mixture into the centre of a banana leaf square, top with sliced tomatoes and fresh lemon basil and fold. Secure with a bamboo skewer.

3. Steam parcels for 10 minutes or grill over very low heat for 7 minutes.

Spiced Tuna Braised in Coconut Milk

(Gulai Masin) West Sumatra

2 stalks lemongrass, crushed

3 kaffir lime leaves, bruised

375 ml seafood stock (page 46)

1 turmeric leaf, bruised

40 g sour starfruits (*blimbing wuluh*), finely sliced (optional lime segments)

800 g tuna loin, cut into 4 steaks, minimum 20-25 mm thick

2 Tbsp tamarind water (see page 69)

100 ml oil for frying

125 ml coconut cream

salt, as needed

100 g cassava leaves, cleaned and blanched for 2 minutes (alternatively use spinach that has been blanched for 10 seconds)

SPICE BLEND

2 Tbsp coconut or vegetable oil

80 g shallots, peeled and sliced

20 g garlic, peeled and sliced

20 g ginger, peeled and sliced

20 g turmeric, peeled and sliced

80 g large red chillies, halved, seeded and sliced

20 g candlenuts, crushed

1. To make the spice blend, combine all ingredients in a stone mortar or food processor and grind into a fine paste.

2. Place ground ingredients into a heavy saucepan. Add lemongrass and lime leaves and sauté over medium heat until fragrant.

3. Fill pan with stock, add turmeric leaf and sour starfruits and simmer over very low heat for 5 minutes. Cool sauce to room temperature.

4. Combine tuna steaks with tamarind water and mix well. Marinate for 30 minutes in refrigerator. *For a better result vacuum pack for 1 hour.*

5. Heat 100 ml oil in frying pan until very hot. Very quickly sear each tuna steak golden on both sides. (This should take less than 20 seconds for one steak. You do not want to cook the steaks. Searing will add a lot of flavour to the dish.) Cool steaks to room temperature and allow oil to drip off.

6. Place two steaks into a foodsafe heatproof plastic bag. Fill sauce equally into the bags. (*Make certain not to wet the area of the bag that will be sealed.*) Seal bags.

7. Vacuum cook at 50°C for 20 minutes (see page 34). Open bags and pour sauce into a saucepan, add coconut cream and quickly bring sauce to simmer. Season to taste with salt.

8. Blend sauce using a hand blender for 15 seconds.

9. Arrange tuna steaks in a serving dish on top of cassava leaves and dress tuna with sauce.

NOTE

Tuna can be replaced with mackerel or any other firm white fish. Finishing the sauce with freshly sliced lemon basil, lime zests and 1 Tbsp lime juice adds a delicious tangy twist to this soupy dish. Be extra careful to keep the temperature as low as possible when cooking tuna as it dries out very quickly. Handle tuna very gently and keep heat as low as possible. Sous vide is the perfect answer to the perfect tuna steak.

Minced Fish Steamed in Banana Leaf
(Otak Otak) *South Sulawesi*

South Sulawesi is known for Coto's various types of beef soups and *otak otak*, and Makassar Ibu Elli is renowned nationwide for serving the best *otak otak*. Up to 10 000 of these delicate fish parcels are prepared daily by a team of ladies that still follow traditional techniques and preparation methods. Most visitors will not only stop by to enjoy a quick snack but will also bring a takeaway box home for their loved ones.

100 ml coconut cream

4 Tbsp sago flour (50 g)

800 g mackerel fillet, skinned and minced

2 Tbsp lime juice

50 g spring onions (scallions), finely sliced

salt, to taste

16 banana leaves, cut into 20-cm squares

SPICE PASTE

100 g shallots, peeled and sliced

30 g garlic, peeled and sliced

3-5 bird's eye chillies, finely sliced

1/2 tsp finely ground white pepper

1. To make the spice paste, combine all ingredients in a stone mortar or food processor and grind into a very fine paste.

2. Combine coconut cream and flour and whisk into a smooth mixture.

3. Combine minced fish, ground spices, coconut-flour mix and blend into a very smooth paste. This is best done using a food processor, as it will take 5–7 minutes before the paste becomes creamy smooth. Add lime juice and spring onions. Season to taste with salt.

4. Place 2 Tbsp (35 g) fish paste in the centre of a banana leaf. Fold the long edges of the banana leaf in towards each other to enclose the filling tightly. Secure the open ends with bamboo skewers. Repeat this process until the ingredients are used up.

5. Steam the parcels for 4 minutes, then place on a charcoal grill and cook for 3 more minutes until the banana leaves are evenly browned.

Steamed Mussels with Rice Cake

(Lontong Kupang) East Java

When buying mollusks, check that they are firmly closed and smell of the ocean. Do not purchase those that show signs of being open. In East Java, where this dish originates from, the tiniest of mussels are used, which makes this dish a rather time-consuming affair. Iced coconut water served by roadside vendors balances this delicate soup so well.

45 ml vegetable or coconut oil

125 ml seafood spice paste (page 40)

2 stalks lemongrass, bruised

3 kaffir lime leaves, bruised

750 mussels or clams, properly cleaned, scraped and washed

400 ml seafood stock (page 46)

50 g leek, sliced into $^1/_2$-cm squares

50 g shallots, sliced into $^1/_2$-cm squares

50 g celery, sliced into $^1/_2$-cm squares

50 g large red chillies, halved, seeded and sliced into $^1/_2$-cm squares

salt, to taste

1 lime for juice

4 Tbsp fried shallots

400 g rice cakes, cut into even slices (page 173)

1. Heat oil in a large saucepan, add spice paste, lemongrass and kaffir lime leaves and sauté until fragrant.

2. Add the dry mussels and continue to sauté over high heat while stirring continuously.

3. Add stock, leek, shallots, celery, red chillies. Mix well, cover and very quickly steam boil the mussels. Keep the lid covered for 2 minutes. This should be enough time for all the shells to open.

4. Season broth with salt and a generous squeeze of lime juice according to taste. Garnish with fried shallots.

5. Serve together with sliced rice cakes.

MEAT

Braised Baby Beef Ribs *(Sampadeh Daging)* West Sumatra

In a typical *Padang* restaurant, all of the bowls of food are laid out in front of customers and the hungry diners need only pay for what they eat. Buffaloes are a symbol of West Sumatra and are used in *rendang*, a rich and spicy buffalo meat or beef dish. Padang food comes from West Sumatra and their restaurant chains can be found throughout Indonesia and neighbouring countries, thus rendering it as probably the most popular regional cuisine of Indonesia. I call it the imperial cusine of Indonesia and when travelling throughout this massive country, one is able to find at least one Padang restaurant in even the most remote village.

SPICE BLEND

75 g shallots, peeled and sliced

30 g garlic, peeled and sliced

100 g galangal (*laos*), peeled and finely sliced

50 g ginger peeled and finely sliced

250 g large red chillies, halved, seeded and sliced

1 tsp cumin

1 litre chicken stock (page 44)

3 salam leaves

3 kaffir lime leaves

1 turmeric leaf

1 stalk lemongrass, bruised

10 sour starfruits, whole (*blimbing wuluh*)

4 Tbsp vegetable oil

1.4 kg baby beef ribs, trimmed

crushed black pepper, to taste

1. To make the spice blend, combine all ingredients in a stone mortar or food processor and grind into a very fine paste. Transfer ground spice blend into a pressure cooker pot. Add stock, all leaves, lemongrass and sour starfruits. Bring to a simmer.

2. Heat 4 Tbsp vegetable oil in a frying pan and quickly sear each beef rib evenly on all sides. Place ribs into simmering stock.

3. Pressure cook ribs at a gauge pressure of 1 bar / 15 psi for 45 minutes (see pages 21-22). Start timing when full pressure is reached. Let the cooker cool for 20 minutes. Lift the ribs from the cooking liquid with a slotted spoon, and transfer to a frying pan.

4. Transfer 250 ml (1 cup) of the cooking liquid to the pan with the ribs, and simmer over very low heat, gently turning and basting the meat for 12–15 minutes until glazed. Reduce the remaining liquid by half and add to the meat. Mix well and simmer for 2 more minutes over low heat.

5. Remove from heat, and let the mixture infuse for 7–10 minutes. Season to taste with crushed black pepper.

Spiced Coconut Beef (*Hagape Daging*) *South Sulawesi*

The highlands of Tanah Toraja serve a similar version of this dish but instead of beef, meat from water buffalos is used instead.

3 Tbsp coconut oil

1 cup freshly grated coconut

3 stalks lemongrass, bruised

1.2 kg beef brisket, cut into 2.5-cm cubes (or beef ribs)

600 ml beef or chicken stock (page 44)

200 ml coconut cream

salt, to taste

crushed black pepper, to taste

roasted coconut, to garnish

SPICE PASTE

3 Tbsp coconut oil

50 g shallots, peeled and sliced

30 g garlic, peeled and sliced

3-5 bird's eye chillies, finely sliced

30 g turmeric, peeled and sliced

30 g galangal (*laos*), peeled and sliced

30 g candlenuts, peeled and sliced

1 tsp coriander seeds, roasted

1/2 tsp caraway seeds

1. Heat 3 Tbsp oil in a non-stick pan over low heat. Add grated coconut and fry gently until golden brown. Set aside to cool before transferring the contents into a stone mortar or food processor and grind coarsely.

2. To make the spice paste, combine all ingredients in a stone mortar or food processor and grind into a fine paste.

3. Place ground ingredients in a heavy saucepan. Add lemongrass and sauté over medium heat until fragrant. Add beef cubes and continue to sauté until the meat changes colour. Add grated coconut and continue to sauté for 2 more minutes. Add stock and mix well. Bring to a boil.

4. Pressure cook at a gauge pressure of 1 bar / 15 psi for 45 minutes (see pages 21-22). Start timing when full pressure is reached. Let the cooker cool for 20 minutes. Lift the meat from the cooking liquid with a slotted spoon, and transfer to a frying pan.

5. Transfer 250 ml (1 cup) of the cooking liquid to the frying pan and simmer over medium heat, gently turning and basting the meat for 12–15 minutes until it is glazed.

6. Combine the remaining liquid with the coconut cream and simmer over low heat until the sauce thickens slightly. Add to frying pan and mix well. Allow the mixture to infuse for 7–10 minutes. There should be very little liquid remaining at the end of this process.

7. Season to taste with salt and crushed black pepper. Garnish with roasted coconut.

Beef Braised with Coconut and Spices

(Rendang Sapi) West Sumatra

3 Tbsp coconut oil

2.4 litres coconut milk

3 stalks lemongrass, bruised

1 turmeric leaf, torn and knotted
   (if turmeric leaf is unavailable, replace
   with 30 g of freshly peeled turmeric
   which you add to the spice paste)

4 kaffir lime leaves, bruised

7 cm cinnamon

1.2 kg beef shoulder or neck, cut into
   2.5-cm cubes brined for 5 hours
   (see page 32)

salt, to taste

SPICE PASTE

80 g shallots, peeled and sliced

50 g garlic, peeled and sliced

120 g large red chillies, halved, seeded
   and sliced

5-7 bird's eye chillies, sliced

50 g galangal (*laos*), peeled and sliced

50 g ginger, peeled and sliced

50 g candlenuts, roasted and crushed

DRY SPICES

1 Tbsp coriander seeds

1 tsp cardamom seeds

1/4 tsp nutmeg, crushed

8 cloves

1/2 tsp white pepper

1. To make the spice paste, combine all ingredients in a stone mortar or food processor and grind into a fine paste. Heat coconut oil in a heavy saucepan, add spice paste and sauté over medium heat until fragrant.

2. To prepare the dry spices combine all ingredients in a stone mortar or food processor and grind into a very fine paste. Combine with the above spice blend.

3. Add coconut milk and blend well. Add lemongrass, turmeric leaf, kaffir lime leaves, and cinnamon. Bring to a simmer. Simmer spice blend over medium heat until the coconut milk becomes very oily and the paste changes to a dark brown colour. This can take up to 1 hour, and the paste should have a creamy, oily consistency.

4. Add beef cubes and bring to a boil. Reduce heat and simmer until meat is tender, stirring frequently, until liquid has almost evaporated and appearance is dry but oily. When cooked there should be almost no liquid left. Season to taste with salt.

NOTE

To learn how to prepare this imperial Indonesian beef dish, I flew across Indonesia to Padang where Pak Dian, a talented and very passionate young chef, taught me the secrets to making this tasty beef dish. It took him two full days to go through the entire process. The meat came from freshly-slaughtered ultra lean old cows, and when we purchased it, the meat was still warm with a very fresh bloody smell. Next the spices were cooked for hours in coconut milk. The milk was first heated, then the spices were added and cooked for hours. During the process the coconut milk gradually broke down and eventually, when all the moisture evaporated, the spices were fried for a seemingly endless time until they looked like a creamy, oily chocolate sauce. After that, the meat was added and the cooking continued for hours and hours. The meat used was so tough that I feared that the simple aluminium wok in which it simmered would disintegrate as a result. However, at the end of the time-consuming cooking process, the dish tasted absolutely delicious.

CONCLUSION

- If you wish to use the ingredients as listed in the note, I would encourage you to use your pressure cooker and follow the steps as described on pages 21-22. If using a pressure cooker, you can replace the coconut milk with 200 ml coconut cream that is added only after the meat comes out of the pressure cooker.
- First sauté the ground spices in 3 Tbsp coconut oil. Next add the beef cubes and continue to sauté until the meat changes colour. Fill cooker with 400 ml beef stock, mix well and bring to a boil.
- Pressure cook at 1 bar / 15 psi for 45 minutes (see pages 21-22). Start timing when full pressure is reached. Let the cooker cool for 20 minutes.
- Lift the meat from the cooking liquid with a slotted spoon, and transfer to a frying pan. Strain the liquid into a pot. Bring to a simmer and skim off as much fat as possible.
- Transfer 250 ml (1 cup) of the cooking liquid to the pan with the beef, and simmer over medium heat, gently turning and basting the meat for 12–15 minutes until it is glazed.
- Combine coconut cream and the remaining liquid and bring to a boil. Reduce sauce to a creamy consistency over low heat.
- Combine sauce and meat and continue to simmer for 2 minutes.
- Remove from heat and let the mixture infuse for 7–10 minutes.
- Season to taste with crushed black pepper.

Braised Beef in Sweet Nutmeg Sauce *(Semur Sapi)* *Central Java*

3 Tbsp coconut oil

20 g palm sugar, chopped

750 ml (3 cups) beef or chicken stock (page 44)

8 Tbsp sweet soy sauce (*kecap manis*)

4 Tbsp salty soy sauce (*kecap asin*)

2 stalks lemongrass, bruised

4 salam leaves

3 kaffir lime leaves

4-6 bird's eye chillies, whole

1 kg beef brisket, sliced 2 x 3 x 1 cm, washed well, drained and dried

300 g potatoes, peeled and cut in 1.5-cm cubes

300 g tomatoes, grilled, peeled, halved and diced

$1/2$ tsp salt

1 Tbsp kaffir lime juice + zest

crushed black pepper, to taste

freshly grated nutmeg, to taste

a handful of finely sliced spring onions (scallions)

3 Tbsp fried shallots

SPICE BLEND

100 g shallots, peeled and sliced

25 g garlic, peeled and sliced

25 g ginger, peeled and sliced

30 g candlenuts, crushed

1 Tbsp crushed black peppercorns

1 Tbsp crushed coriander seeds, roasted

$1/4$ tsp ground nutmeg

$1/4$ tsp crushed cloves

1. To make the spice blend, combine all ingredients in a stone mortar or food processor and grind into a fine paste. Place ground ingredients into a pressure cooker, add oil and palm sugar and sauté over medium heat for approximately 5 minutes or until fragrant.

2. Add stock, both soy sauces, lemongrass, salam and kaffir lime leaves and chillies and bring to a boil, then simmer for 5 minutes over low heat.

3. Add sliced brisket and bring back to a boil. Remove scum, close pressure cover and pressure cook for approximately $1^1/_2$ hours over low heat (see pages 21-22). Remove pot from heat and let it cool for 20 minutes before opening the cover.

4. Strain liquid into a saucepan and reduce to about 500 ml (2 cups).

5. Add potatoes and continue to simmer until potatoes are half-cooked. Add sliced meat and continue to simmer over very low heat until potatoes are cooked, gently turning and basting until glazed and shiny. Add diced tomatoes and mix well.

6. Season to taste with salt, lime juice, lime zests, black crushed pepper and perhaps a little more freshly grated nutmeg.

7. Garnish with spring onions and fried shallots.

Beef Liver Simmered in Spiced Coconut Cream
(Kalio Hati) South Sulawesi

2 Tbsp coconut oil

750 ml beef or chicken stock (page 44)

250 ml coconut cream

7.5 cm cinnamon stick

2 salam leaves

2 kaffir lime leaves

1 turmeric leaf

1 lemongrass, bruised

2 Tbsp tamarind water (see page 69)

1.2 kg beef liver, trimmed and sliced into 50 g steaks

salt, to taste

1 Tbsp lime juice

fried leek, to garnish

SPICE BLEND

250 g large red chillies, halved, seeded and sliced

150 g shallots, peeled and sliced

50 g garlic, peeled and sliced

30 g turmeric, peeled and sliced

30 g ginger, peeled and sliced

50 g galangal (*laos*), peeled and sliced

10 g candlenuts, crushed

DRY SPICES

1 Tbsp crushed coriander seeds

1 tsp ground nutmeg

1 tsp crushed black pepper

1. To make the spice blend, combine all ingredients in a stone mortar or food processor and grind into a very fine paste. Combine dry spices separately in a stone mortar or food processor and grind into a very fine powder.

2. Heat 2 Tbsp coconut oil in a saucepan, add both spice blends and sauté for 2 minutes over low heat until fragrant.

3. Fill pan with stock and coconut cream. Add cinnamon, salam, kaffir lime and turmeric leaves, lemongrass and tamarind water, then simmer for 2 minutes over very low heat.

4. Optional: Cool sauce to room temperature and transfer to a plastic bag to cook liver sous vide at 55°C for 10 minutes or in a ziplock bag in 55°C water bath for 25 minutes (see page 34).

5. Heat remaining oil in a frying pan. Quickly sear each liver steak on both sides and transfer into the sauce. Cook liver for 10 minutes. Lift the meat from the cooking liquid with a slotted spoon. Set aside and keep warm.

6. Bring the cooking liquid back to a simmer and season to taste with salt and 1 Tbsp lime juice. Transfer sauce into a food blender and blend at high speed for 15 seconds or aerate sauce with a hand blender.

7. Pour source over meat and garnish with crispy fried leek.

NOTE

People in Padang love beef and serve it whenever they can. A cheaper alternative is beef intestine. Other intestines can be used with this same recipe. If beef is not available, lamb can be substituted in its place.

Mixed Beef Satay *(Satay Ampet Sasak)* *Lombok*

Although this recipe calls for beef liver and heart, they can be replaced by other cuts of meat or by chicken; chicken heart and liver.

3 Tbsp coconut oil

250 ml beef stock (page 44)

100 ml coconut cream

300 g beef topside, cut into 1.5-cm cubes (a better, more expensive option is the end cut of beef tenderloin or beef sirloin)

300 g beef liver, cut into 1.5-cm cubes

300 g beef heart, cut into 1.5-cm cubes

salt, to taste

red chilli flakes, to taste

1 lime, cut into wedges

SPICE BLEND

40 g shallots, peeled and sliced

30 g garlic, peeled and sliced

40 g ginger, peeled and finely sliced

70 g large red chillies, halved, seeded and sliced

3-5 bird's eye chillies, finely sliced

20 g candlenuts, crushed

1. To make the spice blend, combine all ingredients in a stone mortar or food processor and grind into a very fine paste.

2. Heat oil in a frying pan and sauté ground spices over medium heat until fragrant. Add stock, bring to a boil and simmer for 5 minutes. Add coconut cream, bring back to a boil and simmer until sauce thickens slightly.

3. Divide marinade into three bowls. Season each cut of meat with salt and red chilli flakes.

4. Place into separate bowls of marinade. Mix well, cover and refrigerate for 2 hours.

5. Thread the meat onto *satay* skewers in the following order: topside followed by a piece of heart and then a piece of liver. Combine the remaining marinade in a saucepan, bring back to a simmer and reduce again until the sauce thickens slightly. Season to taste with salt and chilli flakes and a generous squeeze of lime juice.

6. Grill *satay* for only a very short while over very hot charcoal.

Crispy Meat Pancake (*Murtabak*) *West Sumatra*

2 Tbsp vegetable or coconut oil

20 g garlic, peeled and chopped

50 g onion, peeled and chopped not too
fine (optional: shallots)

300 g beef chuck, brisket or topside
or mince using 3-4 mm plate lamb
shoulder or boneless or skinned and
boneless chicken leg

30 g small leek, cleaned, halved and
finely sliced

2-5 bird's eye chillies, finely sliced (adjust
amount according to preference)

1 large red chilli, halved, seeded
and sliced

1 Tbsp curry powder (mild)

4 chicken eggs (optional: duck eggs),
beaten

4 Tbsp finely sliced spring onions
(scallions)

1/4 cup Chinese celery leaves, finely sliced
(optional: fresh coriander, cilantro)

salt and white crushed pepper, to taste

DOUGH

500 g plain all-purpose flour

3 Tbsp coconut oil

180 ml water

1 egg

1 pinch salt

1. To make the filling, heat 2 Tbsp vegetable or coconut oil in a frying pan. Add garlic and onions and sauté over medium heat for 1 minute.

2. Add minced meat, increase heat and continue to sauté until meat changes colour. Add leek and chillies and continue to sauté for 1 more minute. Add curry powder, mix well and sauté for 1 more minute. Set aside and cool.

3. Place minced meat in deep mixing bowl. Add eggs, spring onions, celery; combine well and season to taste with salt and pepper.

4. To make the dough, combine all ingredients and knead into an oily, elastic dough. Cover and leave at room temperature (22°C) for 2 hours.

5. Divide dough into (80 g) portions and roll each into a ball. Similar to a strudel dough, flatten dough on an oiled surface (preferably marble) and pull each side into a square thin sheet measuring about 30 cm in diameter.

6. Place half cup (125 ml) of filling onto the centre of the flattened dough. Fold each side towards the centre, enclosing the filling.

7. To finish the pancakes, heat a generous amount of oil in a frying pan (20 cm in diameter) or griddle. Add the dough-wrapped fillings and fry over medium-high heat on both sides until crispy and golden. While frying, continuously baste with hot oil.

8. Cut into even pieces and serve with vegetable pickles, green bird's eye chillies and a light curry sauce as a dipping.

Murtabak

Murtabak has to be one of Indonesia's most popular street snacks. In every city, every town and the smallest settlements, one can find sellers of this perennial favourite. *Murtabak* originated in Yemen, which has a sizeable Indian population. The word "mutabbaq" in Arabic means "folded". Through Indian traders, *murtabak* has spread back to India and to all parts of Asia. The above recipe originates from Padang in West Sumatra. There is no hard and fast rule as to what type of meat can be used. Simply choose your favourite meat or try fish and shellfish minced and prepare as described. Use your imagination and fill your omelettes with fruits, jam or a little chocolate. Sprinkle your cooked pancake with icing sugar and serve it with your favourite ice cream.

Braised Lamb Shanks with Mushrooms *(Kaki Kambing)* East Java

4 lamb shanks, whole and trimmed,
   400-450 g each, brined for
   12 hours (see page 32)
250 g spice blend for meats (page 40)
4 Tbsp vegetable or coconut oil
1 Tbsp crushed cardamom seeds,
10 cloves, crushed
2 cinnamon sticks, 10-cm long
3 stalks lemongrass, bruised
3 kaffir lime leaves, bruised
500 ml chicken stock (page 44)
250 ml coconut cream
100 g shiitake mushrooms, cleaned
salt, to taste
2 Tbsp lime juice + lime zest

GARNISH
2 Tbsp sliced celery leaves
50 g tomatoes, halved, seeded and diced
2 Tbsp fried shallots
100 g crispy fried leek
50 g *emping* crackers, deep-fried

1. Marinate shanks evenly with 4 Tbsp spice blend.

2. Heat 4 Tbsp oil in a frying pan and evenly brown shanks on all sides. Remove shanks from pan and drain three-quarters of the oil. Add remaining spice blend, cardamom, cloves, cinnamon, lemongrass and kaffir lime leaves and sauté over medium heat until fragrant.

3. Fill pan with stock and bring to a simmer. Transfer liquid to a pressure cooker, add lamb shanks and bring back to simmer. Skim off scum.

4. Pressure cook at a gauge pressure of 1 bar / 15 psi for 40–45 minutes (see pages 21-22). Start timing once full pressure is reached.

5. Turn off the heat and allow the cooker to cool for 20 minutes.

6. Strain two-thirds of the liquid into a saucepan and bring to a quick boil. Remove scum and reduce heat. Add coconut cream, bring back to a boil and simmer for 3 minutes.

7. In a separate saucepan quickly sauté mushrooms in 2 Tbsp oil. Strain sauce over mushrooms, add lamb shanks and remaining sauce and simmer over medium low heat for 12–15 minutes until shanks are glazed and sauce is light and creamy. Remove from heat, and let mixture infuse for 7–10 minutes.

8. With a hand blender, quickly foam up sauce without blending the mushrooms.

9. Season sauce to taste with salt, 2 Tbsp lime juice and lime zest. Garnish dish with celery leaves, diced tomatoes, fried shallots, leek and *emping* crackers.

A Western meal is often named for the pièce de résistance, the cut of meat or the fish or fowl that is featured in the main course, perhaps the sirloin steak, the prime rib, the roast chicken, the fish or perhaps the rack of lamb. The rest of the meal is rather incidental – just something to whet the appetite, to complement the main highlight of the meal, or to provide contrast when the meat has been finished. This practice is not followed in the average Indonesian home. There is no main course. All the food is served on one plate. Rice, which is our main feature sits nicely in the centre. We do not have meat very often as well. The reason for this is simply that meat is expensive. Although Indonesians love meat, the price of meat is simply not for the average person. When you see the large number of animals that wander around or are penned up in the average household backyard, you may wonder why they are not used for food. The answer is straightforward, these animals are much more valuable when used for other purposes.

Sumatran Lamb Curry *(Gulai Kambing)* *West Sumatra*

4 Tbsp coconut oil

10 cm cinnamon stick

750 ml chicken stock (page 44)

4 Tbsp tamarind water

1 turmeric leaf, torn

1 stalk lemongrass, bruised

2 salam leaves

2 lime leaves, torn

1.2 kg lamb shoulder, cut into 2.5-cm cubes and brined for 5 hours (see page 32)

250 ml coconut cream

SPICE PASTE FRESH

60 g shallots, peeled and sliced

30 g garlic, peeled and sliced

4-6 bird's eye chillies, sliced

30 g ginger, peeled and sliced

30 g galangal (*laos*), peeled and sliced

30 g turmeric, peeled and sliced

SPICE PASTE DRY

1 tsp coriander seeds, roasted and crushed

½ tsp peeled and crushed cardamom

½ tsp crushed caraway seeds

¼ tsp ground nutmeg

3 star anise

½ tsp crushed white peppercorns

1. To make fresh spice paste, combine all ingredients in a stone mortar or food processor and grind into a fine paste.

2. To prepare the dry spice paste, combine all ingredients in a different stone mortar or food processor and grind very fine.

3. Heat oil in a heavy saucepan, add both spice blends and cinnamon stick and sauté over medium heat until spices are fragrant and colour changes.

4. Fill saucepan with stock. Add tamarind water, turmeric leaf, lemongrass, salam and lime leaves and bring to a simmer. Reduce heat and simmer for 5 minutes. Add meat, mix well, bring back to a boil and reduce heat. Skim off scum.

5. Pressure cook at a gauge pressure of 1 bar / 15 psi for 25 minutes (see pages 21-22). Start timing when full pressure is reached

6. Let the cooker cool for 20 minutes. Lift the meat from the cooking liquid with a slotted spoon, and transfer to a frying pan.

7 Drain the liquid into a pot. Bring to a simmer and skim off as much fat as possible. Add coconut cream and bring sauce back to a slow boil and simmer until the sauce is lightly creamy.

8. Transfer sauce to the pan with the lamb, mix well and simmer over medium heat. Gently turn and baste the meat for 12–15 minutes until it is glazed, and the dish turns lightly creamy.

9. Remove pan from the heat, and let the mixture infuse for 7–10 minutes. Season to taste with crushed white pepper.

NOTE

If you wish to prepare the dish using chicken, beef, fish or vegetables, follow steps 1-3. For step 4 simply use the protein or vegetable of your choice. If fish is used, add more ginger and tamarind and less dry spices when preparing the spice blend. The cooking time for beef shoulder in a pressure cooker is 1 hour 15 minutes. As for chicken, fish or prawns, vacuum cook in a water bath as described on page 34.

Braised Pork Belly *(Arsik Babi Tapanusli)* *South Sulawesi*

Tana Toraja in the centre of Sulawesi has to be the pork capital of Indonesia. During their colourful cremation ceremonies, a seemingly endless number of black pigs with enormous hanging bellies are sacrificed. Despite the large amounts of fat in this dish, the clever usage of lemongrass, kaffir lime leaves and many other spices give this dish a surprisingly light and nuanced taste. When prepared (as described) in a pressure cooker, the clean flavours of the spices are further enhanced.

1.6 kg pork belly, skin on and cut into 3.5-cm cubes (cubed pork shoulder also works as a leaner alternative)

5 stalks lemongrass, bruised

5 kaffir lime leaves, bruised

60 g ginger, peeled, sliced and crushed

4-6 bird's eye chillies (adjust amount according to preference)

800 ml chicken stock (page 44)

5 Tbsp lime juice

freshly cracked black pepper, to taste

2 Tbsp finely sliced spring onions (scallions)

SPICE PASTE

3 Tbsp coconut oil

60 g shallots, peeled and sliced

30 g garlic, peeled and sliced

80 g large red chillies, halved, seeded and sliced

20 g galangal (*laos*), peeled and sliced

20 g ginger, peeled and sliced

20 g turmeric, peeled and sliced

1. Brine pork belly as explained on page 32 for 6 hours.

2. To make the spice paste, combine all ingredients in a stone mortar or food processor and grind into a fine paste.

3. Transfer spice paste into a pressure cooker pot and sauté over low heat until fragrant. Add pork belly, bruised lemongrass, lime leaves, sliced ginger and bird's eye chillies. Mix well and sauté until meat changes colour. Add chicken stock, mix well and bring to a boil.

4. Pressure cook at a gauge pressure of 1 bar / 15 psi for 45 minutes (see pages 21-22). Start timing when full pressure is reached.

5. Let the cooker cool, or run cool water over the rim, to depressurise it.

6. Lift the meat from the cooking liquid with a slotted spoon, and transfer into the frying pan. Strain the liquid into a pot. Skim off as much fat as possible and reduce liquid by one-third.

7. Transfer 250 ml (1 cup) of the cooking liquid to the frying pan and simmer over medium- high heat, gently turning and basting the meat for 12–15 minutes until it is glazed. Add remaining liquid to pressure cooker pot and bring to a boil.

8. Remove from heat, and let the mixture infuse for 7–10 minutes. Season with lime juice and black pepper.

9. Garnish with spring onions.

Grilled Pork Ribs *(Balung Panggang)* Bali

Balinese people love pork and no ceremony would be a success without it. Grilled pork ribs is without question one of the bestselling dishes on our menu and we often find it difficult to keep up with the demand. Once again, brining for 24 hours and the usage of a pressure cooker does wonders not only to the taste but in this case also to the texture of the ribs. The ribs are then charred over glowing hot charcoal which makes this dish irresistible.

2 Tbsp coconut or vegetable oil

2 stalk lemongrass, bruised

2 kaffir lime leaves, bruised

1 salam leaves

50 ml water

600 ml chicken or pork stock (page 44)

vegetable or coconut oil, as needed

1.2 kg pork ribs, cut in 3 x 3-cm pieces and brined for 24 hours (see page 32)

1 pinch salt, to taste

SPICE BLEND

50 g large red chillies, halved, seeded and sliced

3-5 bird's eye chillies, sliced

50 g shallot, peeled and sliced

30 g garlic, peeled and sliced

25 g galangal (*laos*), peeled and chopped

25 g ginger, peeled and sliced

25 g lesser galangal (*kencur*), washed and sliced

35 g turmeric, peeled and sliced

20 g candlenut, crushed

1/2 tsp dried prawn (shrimp) paste (*terasi*), roasted

1/2 tsp crushed coriander seeds

1/4 tsp crushed black peppercorns

1/4 tsp freshly grated nutmeg

2 cloves, crushed

1. To make the spice blend, combine all ingredients in a stone mortar or food processor and grind into a fine paste.

2. Place ground ingredients in a pressure cooker. Add oil, lemongrass, kaffir lime leaves, salam leaves and water and sauté over medium heat until spice blend is fragrant and shiny-golden in colour. (Reserve 100 g of spice blend for the basting oil). Fill cooker with stock and bring to a simmer.

3. In a frying pan heat 4 Tbsp oil and quickly sear pork ribs on all sides. Transfer ribs to a pressure cooker.

4. Pressure cook at a gauge pressure of 1 bar / 15 psi for 25 minutes (see pages 21-22). Start timing when full pressure is reached.

5. Let the cooker cool for 20 minutes, open cover and allow ribs to completely cool in stock. Lift the ribs from the liquid and allow to dry in an airy place for 1 hour.

6. Combine reserved spice blend with 100 ml vegetable or coconut oil and blend well.

7. Grill ribs over charcoal until golden brown. Frequently turn and baste the ribs.

8. Season to taste with salt.

Braised Pork Shoulder with Eggs *(Lapis Daging)* *Flores*

Next to chickens, pigs are the most common house yard animals in Bali and Flores. They fit into a perfect ecological and economical niche because they eat leftovers or free plant materials that would otherwise go to waste, such as rice bran, banana stems and rotten vegetables from the village market. They are content to live out their lives tied up in a convenient, out of the way place in the house compound, and they require little attention other than considerable food. Furthermore, there is a ready demand for pigs because people in Bali and Flores love to eat them dearly whenever they can afford to. Unfortunately, this is mostly only the case for very special occasions and ceremonies.

3 Tbsp coconut oil

250 g spice blend for meats (page 40)

3 stalks lemongrass, bruised

3 salam leaves

1.2 kg pork shoulder, cut into
   2¹/₂ cm cubes

500 ml chicken stock (page 44)

3 chicken eggs, beaten

salt, to taste

crushed white pepper, to taste

1 Tbsp fried shallots for garnish

1. Heat oil in heavy pressure cooker, add spice paste, lemongrass and salam leaves. Sauté until fragrant.

2. Add pork and continue to sauté until meat is evenly coated with spice paste.

3. Pour chicken stock into the cooker and bring to simmer.

4. Pressure cook at a gauge pressure of 1 bar/15 psi for 25 minutes (see pages 21-22). Start timing when full pressure is reached. Let the cooker cool for 20 minutes.

5. Lift the meat from the cooking liquid with a slotted spoon and transfer to a frying pan.

6. Strain the liquid into a pot, then bring to simmer and skim off as much fat as possible. Reduce liquid down until only 300 ml remains.

7. Transfer cooking liquid to the pan with the pork and mix well. Add the beaten egg and stir while the mixture continues to simmer for 5 more minutes.

8. Season to taste with salt and crushed white pepper, then garnish with fried shallots.

Minced Pork Steamed in Banana Leaf *(Tibu)* Flores

Besides pork, chicken, beef and duck are often prepared using the method explained below. These tasty meat mixtures are stuffed into bamboo tubes and baked over an open fire. As bamboo tubes may not be easy to obtain, we have replaced them with banana leaves in this recipe as they are readily available in most supermarkets.

600 g pork shoulder, minced

200 g pork liver, minced

200 g pumpkin, peeled, diced (³/₄ cm) and blanched

100 g cassava leaves, blanched and chopped (alternative: spinach)

3 Tbsp chopped lemon basil (*kemangi*)

150 g spice blend for meats

salt, to taste

ground white pepper, to taste

12 banana leaf squares, each 12 x 12 cm

1. Combine all ingredients except the banana leaves in a deep mixing bowl and blend into a smooth mixture.

2. Soften each banana leaf wrapper by either holding it over a gas flame or immerse in boiling water for 3 seconds. Top each banana leaf wrapper with 2 Tbsp pork mixture.

3. Take one long edge of the wrapper and fold it in towards the centre to cover the ingredients, and then roll up tightly. Secure open ends with bamboo skewers or toothpicks. Repeat until all ingredients are wrapped in banana leaves.

4. There are a number of ways to cook these tasty parcels: (1) Steam for 7 minutes, (2) Steam for 4 minutes, then place on a charcoal grill and grill for 3 minutes until banana leaves are browned evenly, (3) Grill over very low heat for about 9 minutes, (4) Roast in a 180°C oven for 9 minutes, (5) Place on a hot iron plate or dry frying pan and grill by turning occasionally until done.

Pork Satay (Satay Nuru Ela) *Flores*

Satay is regularly associated with Indonesian and Malaysian cuisine. Most visitors to Indonesia will eat *satay* at their hotels or at restaurants. Hotel *satay* dishes are made with carefully selected, tender, sinew free meat, and often shrimp or lobsters are served. Pair pork *satay* with a creamy peanut sauce (see page 56).

100 ml water

1 stalk lemongrass, bruised

1 salam leaves

800 g pork neck, diced into
    1 x 0.5-cm cubes

200 g spice blend for meat (page 40)

2 Tbsp sweet soy sauce (*kecap manis*)

salt, to taste

bamboo skewers

SPICE PASTE

2 Tbsp vegetable oil

50 g shallots, peeled and sliced

20 g garlic, peeled and sliced

20 g ginger, peeled and sliced

20 g galangal (*laos*), peeled and sliced

20 g turmeric, peeled and sliced

10 g candlenuts, crushed

70 g large red chillies, halved, seeded
    and sliced

2-3 bird's eye chillies, sliced

$1/4$ crushed tsp coriander seeds

2 pinch white pepper corns, crushed

$1/4$ tsp caraway seeds

3 pinch nutmeg, ground

$3/4$ Tbsp salt

1. To make the spice paste, combine all the ingredients in a stone mortar or food processor and grind coarsely. Put aside 100 g for the basting oil.

2. Place the blended ingredients in a saucepan. Add water, lemongrass and salam leaves and simmer over medium heat for approximately 10 minutes or until water has evaporated and marinade changes to a golden colour. Cool before using.

3. To prepare the *satays*, combine meat, spice paste, sweet soy sauce and salt and mix well.

4. Thread 4–6 pieces of meat onto a *satay* skewer and push them together towards one end of the skewer. Repeat until all the meat is used up.

5. Cover *satay* and leave to marinate in the refrigerator for 1 hour.

6. Grill over very hot charcoal until desired doneness is achieved. Baste frequently.

7. For the basting mix, blend 100 g of spice paste with 100 ml coconut oil.

Roast Piglet *(Babi Guling)* Bali

We have taken a slightly different approach with this recipe to cook each and every piece of the pork to perfection while maintaining the traditional flavours of Bali. In this recipe the whole pig is cut into different parts: head, shoulder, belly and the back legs. Next the pork is brined for 24 hours and the various parts roasted at a relatively low temperature (120°C). You may cook the parts at the same time but you must do so with the assistance of a probe. Start with the smallest or thinnest cut and once it reaches a core temperature of 65°C, remove this cut from the oven and allow it to rest on a wire rack in a warm place. Next, insert your probe into the larger piece of roast and when the core temperature of 65°C is reached, remove this piece from the oven as well. Do the same for each cut of meat. Once roasted, allow the meat to rest in a warm spot for approximately 1 hour. Fifteen to 20 minutes prior to serving the pork, return the meat to a very hot oven. This will ensure that the skin is crispy when you serve the roast. If you want a slightly smoky flavour, smoke the meat first before roasting (see page 33).

2 kg pork, boneless with skin on, brined for 24 hours (see page 32)

125 ml turmeric water (very concentrated, see page 61), mixed with 125 ml coconut or vegetable oil

SPICE BLEND

400 g cassava leaves, cleaned, blanched for 5 minutes, and roughly sliced (If cassava leaves are not available, replace with blanched spinach.)

100 g shallots, peeled and sliced

50 g garlic, peeled and sliced

30 g ginger, peeled and chopped

40 g turmeric, peeled and chopped

25 g candlenuts, chopped

30 g galangal (*laos*), peeled and finely chopped

5-7 g bird's eye chillies, finely sliced (adjust amount according to taste)

3 stalks lemongrass, bruised and finely sliced

1/2 Tbsp crushed coriander seeds

1/4 crushed tsp black peppercorns

1/2 tsp dried prawn (shrimp) paste (*terasi*), roasted and crumbed

3 kaffir lime leaves, finely chopped

2 salam leaves

1. To make the spice blend, combine all ingredients and mix thoroughly.

2. Place banana leaves on a perforated square tray or wire rack, top with spice blend and place pork on top (skin up). Place tray on top of a second tray that contains water. This will create a little humidity in the oven during roasting to prevent the roast from drying out.

3. Roast at low temperature (the lower the better, but this will take longer) to a core temperature of 65°C. Brush frequently with turmeric-oil. Allow roast to rest in a warm place for 1 hour.

4. Heat oven to 300°C or higher. Then, 15–20 minutes before serving, return roast back into the oven and sear the skin. This will give you the desired crispy skin within minutes.

5. When serving, first remove the crisp skin with a carving knife or scissors and cut into even pieces. Slice roast evenly. Place spice blend on serving plate, and then top with meat and skin.

Babi Guling in Bali

Balinese people always refer to this dish with the all-purpose word "be" meaning meat. The adjective "guling" is best translated into English as "rotated", or, in the case of cooking, "rotisserie". Basically this dish is simply a cleaned and de-gutted pig stuffed with spices and impaled upon a spit. It is roasted over coals or a low fire by rotating the spit by hand, which often takes hours. Technically the word "guling" refers to anything that is roasted in a rotisserie. The average Balinese person very seldom cooks or eats pork at home, except upon ceremonial occasions. Pigs are large animals, and it would not be practical or economically feasible for a family to slaughter their homegrown pigs for their own consumption. Hence, this dish is only prepared during very special occasions in Bali, such as birthdays, anniversaries or reunions.

POULTRY

Minced Duck Satay (*Satay Bebek Lilit*) *Bali*

If you wish to make *satays* the same way using chicken, pork or seafood, simply follow the directions given and replace the respective protein and the respective spice blend. It is absolutely crucial to only use the freshest meat. Frozen meat will not work as the mince will fall off the skewer.

vegetable oil, as needed
600 g minced duck meat
125 g grated coconut
4 bird's eye chillies, finely chopped
2 Tbsp fried shallots
1 Tbsp fried garlic
1 tsp palm sugar, chopped
salt, to taste
black peppercorns, crushed to taste
bamboo skewers or trimmed lemongrass

SPICE BLEND
60 ml vegetable oil
75 g large red chillies, halved, seeded
  and sliced
75 g shallots, peeled and sliced
50 g garlic, peeled
40 g galangal (*laos*), peeled and sliced
40 g turmeric, peeled and sliced
30 g ginger, peeled and sliced
25 g candlenuts, crushed
$^1/_2$ tsp dried prawn (shrimp) paste (*terasi*),
  roasted
$^1/_2$ tsp crushed coriander seeds
1 pinch black peppercorns, crushed
1 pinch nutmeg, ground
2 cloves

1. To make the spice blend, combine all ingredients in a stone mortar or food processor and grind into a fine paste.

2. Heat oil in a heavy saucepan. Add ground spices and sauté over low heat until fragrant and colour changes. Set aside to cool. Reserve 100 g spice blend for the salad.

3. Combine minced duck, grated coconut, 4 Tbsp spice paste, bird's eye chillies, fried shallots, fried garlic, palm sugar, salt and peppercorns. Mix well into a smooth paste.

4. Using 1 heaped tablespoon full of this mixture, mould it around a wooden skewer or over the trimmed bulbous end of a lemon grass stalk.

5. Grill over very hot charcoal until golden brown, basting frequently with a basting mix made from 2 Tbsp of the reserved spice paste and 2 Tbsp vegetable oil.

Balinese Duck Curry (*Bebek Menyatnyat*) *Bali*

Duck is a great favourite on festive occasions in Bali. Note that chicken can be used as a substitute for duck if preferred. The cooking method described in this recipe is suitable for ducks with relatively tough meat such as those found in the Bali rice fields. It can be adapted for goose meat as well.

1 whole duck, weighing about 2 kg, cut in half and deboned, leave in leg bone, but cut open to cook evenly through

4 Tbsp vegetable or coconut oil

200 g spice blend for meat (page 40)

2 stalks lemongrass, bruised

2 kaffir lime leaves, bruised

2 salam leaves

400 ml chicken stock (page 44)

100 ml coconut cream

salt, to taste

black peppercorns, to taste

limes and lime zest, to taste

1. Brine duck for 6 hours (see page 32)

2. Heat 4 Tbsp vegetable or coconut oil in a nonstick pan. Sear duck very quickly on both sides for 30 seconds. Drain oil, leaving 1 tablespoon in the pan.

3. Add spice blend, lemongrass, kaffir lime leaves, salam leaves and sauté over medium heat for 2 minutes until fragrant.

4. Fill pan with stock and bring to a boil. Reduce heat and simmer for 2 minutes.

5. Transfer duck and sauce into a pressure cooker and pressure cook at a gauge pressure of 1 bar / 15 psi for 25 minutes (see pages 21-22). Start timing when full pressure is reached.

6. Turn off heat and let the cooker cool for 20 minutes. Remove the duck from the cooking liquid with a slotted spoon, and set aside in a warm place.

7. Strain the liquid into a pot. Bring to a simmer and skim off as much fat as possible.

8. Add coconut cream and bring back to a simmer. Add the duck and simmer over medium to low heat, gently turning and basting the meat for 12–15 minutes until it is glazed and the sauce lightly thickens. Season to taste with salt, pepper and a generous squeeze of lime juice and some lime zest.

A GREAT OPTION
Simmer the duck for 17–20 minutes, then lift the duck from the sauce and allow the skin to dry in a warm place for 30 minutes. Heat 4 Tbsp vegetable or coconut oil until very hot, then quickly sear the duck for 30 seconds. This process will add a delicious roasted flavour to the duck.

Chicken and Vegetable Hot Pot
(Sosok Utan) South Sulawesi

This recipe calls for a little bit of extra work with the chicken prior to cooking. The chicken has to be completely deboned, which you can ask your local butcher to do. The chicken then has to be brined for a good 5 hours and the actual cooking will take close to an hour. However, if you prepare well in advance and follow the steps as explained, you will be amply rewarded with an incredibly delicious dish. Take extra care when preparing the chicken stock as described on page 44. To further enhance the flavour, we recommend preparing one of the various chilli sambals from the south of Sulawesi (page 61).

1.2-1.4 kg whole chicken, opened butterfly, backbone removed, and cut into 8 pieces. Remove all the bones.

1.2 litres chicken stock (page 44)

4 Tbsp oil

2 stalks lemongrass, bruised

3 kaffir lime leaves, torn

300 g pumpkin, cut into ¾-cm cubes

200 g sweet corn kernels, blanched

100 g spinach, cleaned

4 Tbsp finely sliced lemon basil (*kemangi*)

salt, to taste

ground white pepper, to taste

SPICE PASTE

3 Tbsp vegetable oil

50 g garlic, peeled and sliced

½ tsp dried prawn (shrimp) paste (*terasi*), roasted

¼ tsp crushed white pepper

5-7 bird's eye chillies, finely sliced

1. Brine chicken pieces for 5 hours. See page 32 for directions.

2. To make the spice paste, combine all ingredients in a stone mortar or food processor and grind into a very fine paste.

3. Transfer the spice paste into a soup pot. Add 3 Tbsp stock and sauté over medium heat until fragrant. Cool. Take one-third of the spice blend and evenly marinate all chicken pieces.

4. In a non-stick pan, heat 4 Tbsp oil and quickly sear chicken pieces until they are lightly golden on both sides. This will add a lot of delicious chicken flavour to the dish. Cool the chicken to room temperature and vacuum seal in heat-resistant plastic bags. Vacuum cook chicken at 65°C for 50 minutes (see page 34). Reserve liquid in the bag for the soup.

5. In soup pot, heat remaining two-thirds of spice blend, add lemongrass and kaffir lime leaves and sauté until fragrant. Add pumpkin and continue to sauté until pumpkins are evenly coated.

6. Fill soup pot with remaining chicken stock and bring to a boil. Simmer until the pumpkin is three-quarters soft. Add sweet corn and continue to simmer until the pumpkin is almost soft. Add spinach and bring back to a simmer.

7. Place the chicken pieces back in the broth, bring back to a simmer and season to taste with sliced lemon basil, salt and white pepper.

Chicken in Spiced Coconut Milk *(Be Siap Base Kalas)* *Bali*

1.2 kg chicken leg, deboned and
    cut into 2 ^{1}/2-cm cubes
250 g chicken spice paste (page 40)
30 ml coconut oil
2 stalks lemongrass, bruised
3 kaffir lime leaves, bruised
1 salam leaf
300 ml chicken stock (page 44)
125 ml coconut cream
salt, to taste
juice of 1 lime, to taste

GARNISH
lime zest
sliced lemons

1. Combine the chicken with 125 g chicken spice paste and blend well (optional: vacuum pack chicken into two heatproof plastic pouches).

2. Heat oil in a heavy saucepan. Add remaining spice paste, lemongrass, kaffir lime and salam leaves and sauté for 2 minutes over low heat until fragrant.

3. Add meat and continue to sauté for 2 minutes, or until meat has changed colour (optional: heat water bath to 65°C and vacuum cook chicken for 20 minutes).

4. Fill the saucepan with chicken stock, blend well and bring to a simmer for 2 minutes. Add coconut cream, mix well and bring very slowly to a simmer. Reduce heat to 65° C and allow chicken to cook for 7 minutes.

5. Season with salt to taste and the juice of 1 lime. Garnish with lime zest and sliced lemon.

NOTE ON VACUUM COOKING
- Vacuum pack marinated chicken into two heatproof plastic pouches.
- Heat water bath to 65°C and vacuum cook chicken for 20 minutes (see page 34).
- To make the sauce, heat oil in a heavy saucepan; add remaining 125 g spice paste, 4 lemongrass, kaffir lime and salam leaves and sauté for 2 minutes over low heat until fragrant.
- Fill the saucepan with chicken stock, blend well and bring to a simmer for 2 minutes. Add coconut cream, mix well and bring very slowly to a simmer. Reduce heat and simmer sauce until lightly creamy.
- Take the meat out of the plastic pouches and add to sauce, blending well. Over very low heat, simmer the dish for 2 more minutes, gently turning and basting meat.
- Season to taste with salt, lime zest and a generous amount of lime juice, and sliced lemon basil.

Fried Chicken *(Manuk Goreng Khas Taliwang)* Nusa Tenggara Barat

4 spring chickens, 800 g each, opened butterfly-style and completely deboned

2 stalks lemongrass, bruised

4 salam leaves

3 kaffir lime leaves

750 ml chicken stock (page 44)

250 ml coconut cream

salt, to taste

1 Tbsp lime juice

4 Tbsp rice flour

oil for frying

SPICE PASTE

3 Tbsp coconut oil

$1/4$ tsp black pepper

5-7 bird's eye chillies, sliced

70 g large red chillies, halved, seeded and sliced

70 g shallots, peeled and sliced

50 g garlic, peeled and sliced

40 g ginger, peeled and sliced

40 g galangal (*laos*), peeled and sliced

40 g turmeric, peeled and sliced

1 tsp palm sugar

1 tsp dried prawn (shrimp) paste, roasted

1. Brine chicken for 6 hours (see page 32). Keep refrigerated for 4 hours, and the final 2 hours at room temperature.

2. To make the spice paste, combine all ingredients in a stone mortar or food processor and grind into a fine paste. Transfer ground spices into a heavy saucepan, add lemongrass, salam and lime leaves and slowly heat until spices are fragrant and soft. Reserve one-quarter cup of spice paste for basting.

3. Fill the saucepan with chicken stock, bring back to a boil and simmer for 10 minutes. Add coconut cream and bring back to a simmer. Season to taste with salt. Allow sauce to cool. Add 1 Tbsp lime juice.

4. Vacuum cook chicken or cook in a ziplock bag at 65°C for 50 minutes (see page 34). Remove chicken from cooking liquid and place on a rack and allow it to rest for 45 minutes. (This will allow the skin to dry and turn golden crispy when fried or grilled.)

5. Bring cooking liquid back to a boil and reduce until the sauce thickens and the coconut cream starts to break down.

6. Combine the reserved spice paste with an equal amount of coconut or vegetable oil. Evenly brush chicken pieces with this marinade.

7. Dust chicken evenly with rice flour and deep-fry over high heat (180°C) until golden brown. This should only take 2 minutes. Drain on paper towel.

8. Serve with rice and garnish as desired.

Lombok Grilled Chicken

(Ayam Taliwang) Nusa Tenggara Barat

4 spring chickens, 800 g each, opened butterfly-style and completely deboned

2 stalks lemongrass, bruised

4 salam leaves

3 kaffir lime leaves

750 ml chicken stock (page 44)

250 ml coconut cream

salt, to taste

1 Tbsp lime juice

oil for frying

SPICE PASTE

3 Tbsp coconut oil

¼ tsp black pepper

5-7 bird's eye chillies sliced

70 g large red chillies, halved, seeded and sliced

70 g shallots, peeled and sliced

50 g garlic, peeled and sliced

40 g ginger, peeled and sliced

40 g galangal (laos), peeled and sliced

40 g turmeric, peeled and sliced

1 tsp palm sugar

1 tsp prawn (shrimp) cake, roasted

1. Brine chicken for 6 hours (see page 32). Keep refrigerated for 4 hours, and the final 2 hours at room temperature.

2. To make the spice paste, combine all ingredients in a stone mortar or food processor and grind into a fine paste. Transfer ground spices into a heavy saucepan, add lemongrass, salam and lime leaves and slowly heat until spices are fragrant and soft. Reserve one-quarter cup of spice paste for basting.

3. Fill the saucepan with chicken stock, bring back to a boil and simmer for 10 minutes. Add coconut cream and bring back to a simmer. Season to taste with salt. Allow sauce to cool. Add 1 Tbsp lime juice.

4. Place each chicken into a vacuum bag. Add 100 ml of sauce and vacuum seal the bags.

5. Vacuum cook chicken or cook in a ziplock bag at 65°C for 50 minutes (see page 34). Remove chicken from cooking liquid and place on a rack and allow it to rest for 45 minutes. (This will allow the skin to dry and turn golden crispy when fried or grilled.)

6. Bring cooking liquid back to a boil and reduce until the sauce thickens and the coconut cream starts to break down.

7. Combine the reserved spice paste with an equal amount of coconut or vegetable oil. Evenly brush chicken pieces with this marinade.

8. Grill the chicken over very hot glowing charcoals until golden brown. Baste frequently with basting mix on both sides to prevent the chicken from burning and to give the chicken a golden, shiny colour.

9. Serve with steamed rice and garnish as desired.

NOTE
By adding 3 tablespoons of honey to your basting mix, you add a delicious flavour to this delicate dish.

Roast Chicken in Banana Leaf (*Ayam Betutu*) *Bali*

A digital thermometer in your kitchen is essential as it allows you to monitor and check the core temperature of meats. It is an incredibly useful tool and takes the guesswork out of your cooking, especially when using the steamer to cook wrapped food. Set the core temperature at 65°C in your gadget and steam for as long as it takes to reach 65°C. Allow the wrapped food to rest for 45 minutes in a warm place before opening the layers of banana leaf and searing the basted chicken in a very hot oven.

1 whole chicken, weighing about
    1.2-1.5 kg and brined for 12 hours
    (see page 32)

200 g cassava leaves, cleaned and
    blanched for 3 minutes, drained and
    roughly chopped. Alternatively, use
    spinach leaves that have been
    blanched for 15 seconds.

5 kaffir lime leaves, finely sliced

2 salam leaves

banana leaves, greaseproof paper
    or aluminium foil for wrapping

SPICE BLEND

[Alternatively use 250 g spice blend
    for meat (page 40)]

50 g shallots, peeled and sliced

25 g garlic, peeled and sliced

50 g turmeric, peeled and chopped

25 g lesser galangal (*kencur*), washed
    and chopped

30 g ginger, peeled and chopped

25 g galangal (*laos*), peeled and chopped

80 g large red chillies, halved, seeded
    and sliced

5 bird's eye chillies, sliced

25 g candlenuts, crushed

4 stalks lemongrass, bruised and
    finely sliced

20 g palm sugar, chopped

1 tsp crushed coriander seeds

1 pinch salt

1 pinch crushed black peppercorns

2 Tbsp vegetable or coconut oil

1. Ensure that both the inside and outside of the chicken are completely cleaned and thoroughly rinsed after brining. Dry with towel and season both the inside and outside of the chicken with salt and pepper.

2. To make the spice blend, combine all ingredients in a stone mortar or food processor and grind into a fine paste. Set 75 g of the spice blend aside to blend with 75 ml of vegetable or coconut oil to make a basting mix.

3. Combine the rest of the spice mix with cassava leaves, kaffir lime and salam leaves and mix well. Season to taste with salt and pepper.

4. Loosen the skin from the chicken breast without breaking it and stuff half of the cassava spice blend between the skin and the chicken breast. Fill the centre of the chicken with the remainder of the spice blend and enclose with a *satay* skewer.

5. Wrap the chicken in several layers of banana leaves, greaseproof paper or foil and steam to a core temperature of 65°C. Allow it to rest in a warm place for 45 minutes.

6. Open upper layers of banana leaves to expose chicken breast and legs. Baste with basting mix and transfer the chicken onto a wire rack in a very hot oven (275°C) and sear for 10–15 minutes. This will result in golden crispy skin.

7. Remove the banana leaves, cut the chicken meat into small pieces and serve with the spice blend.

Fried Tempeh with Chicken Ragout

(Sambal Goreng Tempeh dan Tekokak) *Flores*

Tempeh is very common throughout Flores. It is a cake made from boiled, hulled and skinned soybeans. It is not complicated to make tempeh at home – simply follow the steps as described on page 164.

oil, as needed

200 g fermented soybean cake *tempeh*, cut into equal pieces (page 164)

rice flour to dust soybean cake for frying

3 Tbsp vegetable or coconut oil

50 g shallots, peeled and sliced

30 g garlic, peeled and sliced

50 g large green chillies, halved, seeded and sliced

50 g large red chillies, halved, seeded and sliced

3-5 bird's eye chillies, sliced

1 stalk lemongrass, bruised

1 salam leaf

150 g chicken leg, deboned, diced and seasoned with salt and white ground pepper

150 g chicken liver, cleaned and seasoned with white ground pepper

3 Tbsp sweet soy sauce (*kecap manis*)

2 Tbsp salty soya sauce (*kecap asin*)

5 Tbsp chicken stock (page 44)

salt, to taste

ground white pepper, to taste

1. Heat sufficient oil to deep-fry soybean cakes (150°C). Fry the flour-dusted soybean cake pieces until golden and crispy. Gradually increase heat. Drain on absorbent paper towels.

2. Heat oil in a frying pan and add shallots, garlic, chillies, lemongrass and salam leaves. Sauté until fragrant.

3. In a separate frying pan, heat 2 Tbsp vegetable or coconut oil until very hot. Add diced chicken meat and stir-fry for 30 seconds. Add chicken livers and continue to stir-fry for an additional minute. Combine sautéed spices, meat, liver and soy sauce and continue to stir-fry for 1 minute. Add stock and simmer for $1/2$ minute longer while continuously stirring.

4. Season to taste with salt and ground white pepper. Serve chicken ragout over crispy fried soybean cakes.

VEGETABLES
& TEMPEH

SOYBEANS IN TOFU & TEMPEH

Discovered in the 15th century BC, the soybean has evolved from its humble beginning in the East to become one of the most sought after food in the world today.

Considered a balanced food, each soybean contains proteins, carbohydrates, vitamins, minerals, fibre and fat—all nutrients essential to human health. Eaten on its own or in combination with other foods, soybeans can provide a high-quality, nutrient-dense meal. It is this balance and versatility that has made the soybean an important component in the human diet.

TOFU

Tofu is a soft cake made from soybean curds. The soybeans are thoroughly washed and then soaked for about 3 hours. Next with the skin on, they are fed into an electrical grinder that reduces them into very fine pulp. Water is continuously added during the grinding process. This pulp is then boiled for about 45 minutes using the remaining liquid from the previous batch of tofu. The solids are then filtered using a large cotton cloth, which is similar to the process of making cheese. The wad of wet pulp is placed in the cloth and wrung out until the residue is almost dry. Next, vinegar (Nigari) is added to the liquid that has passed

through the filter. This causes the curds to precipitate. The liquid is stirred while the curds are forming. The solids are then separated through a mousseline cloth, and wrung out until the residue is almost dry. The curds are now poured into a shallow cloth-lined rectangular wooden mould and the water is then squeezed out of the wet curds. A heavy board is placed on top of the mould and it presses the curds down to form a large, white, cheese-like cake.

Soybean Curd Tofu

1 kg soybeans, thoroughly washed, cleaned and drained

5.5 litres water

40 g Nigari (available in Japanese food stores), dissolved in one cup of water

200 ml turmeric water (page 61)

½ Tbsp finely crushed black pepper

¼ tsp crushed nutmeg

12 cm cinnamon stick (optional)

2 Tbsp chopped lemon basil

40 g salt

1. Soak the dried soybeans in 4 litres water at 25°C for 3 hours.

2. Grind soybeans in batches in a food processor or blender with the water they were soaked in.

3. In a large pot, bring 4 litres of water to a boil and add the ground soybeans.

4. Strain the hot mixture through a colander lined with a finely woven cotton cloth.

5. Carefully gather up the sides of your cloth and twist it together. Squeeze out as much soymilk as possible. Keep squeezing as hard as you can in order to extract every bit of moisture from the bean pulp.

6. In a cup, combine Nigari mixture with 1 cup water and stir until dissolved.

7. Rinse cooking pot and place back on the stove. Transfer the soymilk to the pot. Add turmeric water, black pepper, nutmeg, cinnamon, lemon basil and salt, then reheat, stirring continuously with a wooden spatula. Remove pot from heat when the soymilk is between 65°C-68°C.

8. Add half of the Nigari mixture to the soymilk, stirring with a spatula in a whirlwind pattern. Bring spoon to a halt upright in the soymilk after stirring vigorously 5–6 times and wait until the mixture stops spinning. Add the remaining Nigari mixture and stir gently in a figure eight pattern. When the soymilk starts to coagulate, cover pot and let it sit for 15 minutes.

9. Line a colander with a clean and tightly woven cotton cloth. Set the colander over a bowl that can support it. With a soup ladle, gently transfer the coagulated soymilk into the cloth-lined colander.

10. Fold the cloth over the top of the coagulated soymilk. Place a square board on top and a weight of about 3-4 kg on it and allow to stand for about 30 minutes. This process presses out excess water and makes the tofu firm.

11. Remove pressed curd from board after 30 minutes and cut into even squares. Immerse in water and store in refrigerator until needed.

TEMPEH

Tempeh is a type of fermented soybean cake made from boiled, hulled and skinned soybeans. The texture of the cake is soft but firm, and it is normally prepared by cutting into thin slices and frying until golden brown. Tempeh can be served as a side dish along with rice or as a snack.

To make *tempeh*, a special variety of mould or *tempeh* yeast is added to soybeans and left to ferment. At the end of the fermentation period, the mould tendrils, technically called mycelia, will entwine the beans, forming a reasonably firm cake.

The ideal temperature for fermentation is between 25°C and 28°C. For cooler temperatures, more yeast can be added, but it is usually about 1 Tbsp *tempeh* yeast for every 50 kg of soybeans.

In Indonesia, the process starts with wrapping soybeans in hibiscus leaves which naturally contain the desired rhizopus spores to encourage the growth of mould.

Tempeh Starter

200 g soybeans
Hibiscus leaves (*daun waru*),
    as needed, thoroughly washed,
    cleaned and dried

1. Thoroughly wash soybeans to remove impurities and as much skin as possible. Soak for 24 hours.

2. Boil soybeans in water until tender.

3. Drain beans and remove skins. Leave to cool to room temperature.

4. Line a wire rack with cheesecloth and arrange half the hibiscus leaves over the cheesecloth. Separate soybeans into two equal amounts and place them 0.5-cm apart on hibiscus leaves. Cover beans with remaining hibiscus leaves and place another cheesecloth over them.

5. Leave in a dark and humid room, ideally between 26°C and 28°C, for 3 days. You should see a healthy growth of mould. The mouldy beans can then be added to the soybeans to facilitate the fermentation process.

Javanese *Tempeh*

2 kg soybeans
1 tsp *tempeh* starter

1. Thoroughly wash soybeans to remove impurities and as much skin as possible.

2. Transfer to a pot and pour boiling water over. Mix well and leave to soak for 1 hour. While soaking, mix the beans frequently and remove as much skin as possible.

3. Drain and soak the beans in fresh cold water for 24 hours. Replace the water every 5 hours. With each change of water, rinse and remove as much skin as possible.

4. Fill a pot with three times as much water as soybeans and bring to a boil. Add the soaked soybeans and bring to a boil over high heat. Boil the beans until tender and all the skins have detached. This can take up to 2 hours.

5. Discard water and skins. Place the beans on a cheesecloth over a flat surface and leave to dry and cool to room temperature. This will take about 1 hour.

6. Sprinkle the starter evenly over the beans and mix thoroughly. Wear plastic gloves if possible.

7. Pack 100 g of beans into individual plastic bags. Seal the bags by rolling up the open end and fastening with staples. Poke a hole at every 1.5-cm interval to allow air to enter and help the fermentation process.

8. Arrange the bags neatly onto a wire rack and store in a dark and humid room, ideally between 25°C and 28°C. Leave to ferment for 2 days.

Creamy Vegetable Stew with Fried Tofu

(Sayur Mesanten dan Tahu Goreng) Bali

Any type of vegetable can be used for this dish. If tofu is not to your taste, then serve
this creamy delight with any grilled meat, chicken or fish.

45 ml vegetable or coconut oil

125 g vegetable spice paste (page 40)

2 stalks lemongrass, bruised

3 kaffir lime leaves, bruised

375 ml vegetable stock (page 47)

125 ml coconut cream

100 g green beans, cut evenly
($2^1/_2$ cm long) and blanched

100 g corn kernels, blanched

50 g petai, blanched

50 g shiitake mushrooms, sliced

75 g tomatoes or cherry tomatoes, peeled
(large tomatoes seeded and sliced,
cherry tomatoes halved)

salt, to taste

lime juice + zest, to taste

8 pieces tofu, 80 g each, cut into halves
(page 163)

50 g rice flour

250 g frying batter (page 29)

2 Tbsp lemon basil (*kemangi*), finely sliced

1. Heat oil in a saucepan. Add spice paste, lemongrass and kaffir
   lime leaves and sauté over low heat until fragrant.

2. Fill the saucepan with stock and coconut cream and bring
   to a simmer.

3. Add all vegetables except for tomatoes and simmer for
   3 minutes until the sauce turns lightly creamy.

4. Add tomatoes, mix well and season sauce to taste with salt,
   lime juice and zest.

5. Dust the tofu with rice flour, then dip them into the batter
   and fry until golden (page 29). Drain on paper napkin.

6. Serve with lots of finely sliced lemon basil.

Fried Tofu with Seafood Filling *(Tahu Isi)* *Bali*

If you prefer to fill your tofu with meat or chicken, follow the same recipe for the filling but replace the fish with your choice of meat and the respective spice blend. As with anything deep-fried, using moderately hot oil will result in beautiful crispy skin.

4 tofu, 100 g each, cut into even
    triangles (page 163)

100 g vegetable spice blend (page 40)

100 ml vegetable stock (page 47)

50 g rice flour

250 g frying batter (page 29)

oil for deep frying

FILLING

300 g fish fillet, finely minced (any firm
    fish will work as well)

125 g freshly grated coconut

60 ml coconut cream

100 g seafood spice blend (page 40)

2-4 bird's eye chillies, very finely chopped

3 kaffir lime leaves, finely chopped

1 pinch black peppercorns, finely
    crushed

1 pinch salt

1 tsp palm sugar

SAUCE

100 g vegetable spice blend (page 40)

100 ml vegetable stock (page 47)

50 ml coconut cream

1 kaffir lime leaf, bruised

salt and pepper, to taste

1 lime (use the rind for zest and its
    fruit for juice)

1. To make the filling, combine all ingredients and mix into a homogeneous sticky paste.

2. Cut pockets into the centre of the tofu and fill with seafood filling.

3. Combine 100 g vegetable spice blend and 100 ml vegetable stock in a saucepan and quickly bring to a boil. Cool to room temperature. Marinate tofu for 1 hour with this marinade, turning the tofu every 5 minutes.

4. Drain excess marinade and dust tofu evenly with rice flour. Coat pockets evenly with frying batter.

5. Deep-fry in medium-hot oil (140°C-150°C) until golden crispy.

6. To make the sauce combine vegetable spice blend, vegetable stock, coconut cream and kaffir lime leaf in a saucepan and quickly bring to a boil. Simmer for 1 minute. Blend using a hand blender for 30 seconds. Season to taste with salt, pepper, lime zest and lime juice.

Fried Tofu with Sliced Tomatoes *(Tahu Goreng Tomat)* *Flores*

Tofu and *tempeh* are relatively recent introductions to the diet of those living in the rural areas of Flores. Most *tempeh* and tofu are produced in Labuhanbajo or Ruteng and then delivered daily to the regional markets in more remote areas. As these markets rotate daily from village to village, fresh soybean products are available only once a week. Due to the distance away from the production centres, the prices are much higher than those in the big towns and too expensive for the ordinary family.

4 firm pieces of tofu, each approximately 100 g (page 163)

2 Tbsp rice flour or cassava flour

oil for frying

salt, to taste

crushed white pepper, to taste

a handful of lemon basil

a handful of spring onions

DRESSING

4 Tbsp vegetable oil

60 g shallots, peeled and sliced

200 g tomatoes, peeled, halved, seeded, and diced or sliced

1 Tbsp palm sugar

5-7 bird's eye chillies, finely sliced

1 Tbsp tamarind water (see page 69)

2 Tbsp lime juice

4 Tbsp roughly chopped lemon basil (*kemangi*)

1. Dust tofu evenly with rice flour.

2. Deep fry in medium-hot oil (150°C) until golden crispy. Drain on paper napkin.

3. To make the dressing, heat oil in a saucepan and add shallots. Sauté until fragrant. Remove from heat and cool. Add the remaining ingredients and blend well. Season to taste with salt and crushed white pepper.

4. Garnish with sprigs of lemon basil and spring onions.

Grilled Eggplants in Tomato Coconut Sauce
(Terong Santen) Maluku

This is the perfect condiment to anything grilled. If eaten on its own, then steamed rice cakes or fried *krupuks* make the perfect condiment. Vegetarians love this dish and in the Malukus, many people enjoy this tasty treat for breakfast.

200 ml vegetable or chicken stock (page 47 or 44)

100 ml coconut cream

200 g tomatoes, grilled, peeled, seeded and diced (keep the juice)

8 eggplants, cut into halves lengthwise

1 Tbsp salt + more to taste

4 Tbsp coconut oil

salt, to taste

¹/₄ tsp crushed white peppercorns

3 Tbsp finely sliced lemon basil (kemangi)

SPICE PASTE

2 Tbsp coconut oil

50 g shallots, peeled and sliced

30 g garlic, peeled and sliced

75 g large red chillies, halved, seeded and sliced

5-7 bird's eye chillies, finely sliced

30 g turmeric, peeled, sliced and finely chopped

30 g ginger, peeled, sliced and finely chopped

1. To make the spice paste, combine all ingredients in a stone mortar or food processor and grind into a fine paste. Transfer ground spice paste into a saucepan and sauté for 2 minutes until fragrant.

2. Fill the saucepan with stock and coconut cream. Bring to a boil and simmer over low heat for 5 minutes. Add tomatoes, bring back to a boil and simmer for 1 more minute. Season to taste with salt, white crushed pepper and lime juice.

3. To prepare the eggplants, combine 1 Tbsp salt and 4 Tbsp coconut oil and blend well. Brush each of the eggplant halves evenly with this salt-oil marinade and set aside for 10 minutes.

4. Grill the eggplants over medium-hot charcoal or bake in the oven until the eggplants are soft and their skin comes off easily.

5. Place two eggplant halves into the centre of a plate and cover with sauce. Garnish with lemon basil.

Vegetables in Spiced Chilli Dressing

(Pelecing Sayur) Nusa Tenggara Barat

This healthy but delectable dressing can be paired with grilled fish or chicken.
Any vegetable can be blended with this rather spicy sauce.

200 g water spinach, cleaned, cut into
    2.5-cm lengths and blanched

100 g fern tips, cleaned and blanched

50 g bean sprouts, blanched

100 g small green beans, cleaned
    and blanched

50 g peanuts with skin, deep-fried or
    roasted golden brown, then roughly
    crushed

CHILLI TOMATO SAMBAL

3-5 bird's eye chillies, finely sliced

1 tomato, grilled, skinned and seeded

1/2 Tbsp dried prawn (shrimp) paste,
    roasted

3 Tbsp vegetable or chicken stock
    (page 47 or 44)

salt, to taste

COCONUT SAMBAL

3 Tbsp coconut oil

2 large red chillies, grilled, skin and
    seeds removed

60 g shallots, grilled

40 g garlic, grilled

1 Tbsp lime juice + more to taste

1 tsp palm sugar

100 g coconut with skin, roasted brown
    and grated with a vegetable shredder

salt, to taste

1. Prepare chilli tomato sambal. Combine all ingredients in a stone mortar or food processor and grind into a paste. Season to taste with salt and adjust amount of water if necessary. Set aside.

2. Prepare coconut sambal. Combine all ingredients except grated coconut in a stone mortar or food processor and grind into a smooth sauce. Blend with grated coconut and season to taste with salt and more lime juice.

3. Bring a pot of water to the boil and blanch water spinach, fern tips, bean sprouts, and green beans separately. Drain well and place in a large bowl. Add chilli tomato sambal and coconut sambal and toss well.

4. Garnish with roasted peanuts. Serve.

NOTE
Blanch vegetables just before serving and for less than a minute in rapidly boiling water. Drain well and allow steam from the vegetables to evaporate. Serving vegetables warm will greatly enhance the flavour of both dressings. This simple vegetable dish is a delectable condiment when served with grilled fish or grilled chicken.

Fried Rice with Noodles *(Nasi Goreng Mawut)* *East Java*

Although it is not often cooked in a private home for local consumption, *nasi goreng* is a very popular street food treat for Indonesian people and is found almost everywhere. The dish is often topped with a fried egg.

4 Tbsp vegetable or coconut oil

100 g chicken thighs, deboned, skinned, and cut into 1-cm cubes

2 Tbsp meat spice blend (page 40)

100 g prawns (shrimps), peeled, cleaned, deveined and cut into 1-cm cubes

2 Tbsp seafood spice blend (page 40)

4 Tbsp vegetable or coconut oil

50 g white cabbage, sliced

20 g large red chillies, halved, seeded and sliced

3-5 bird's eye chillies, finely sliced

1 Tbsp chilli sauce (pick your favourite between page 58 to 63)

2 Tbsp salty soy sauce (*kecap asin*)

50 g shiitake mushrooms, sliced

3 eggs, blended thoroughly

300 g rice, cooked and cooled

300 g egg noodles, boiled and cooled

30 g spinach, cleaned and roughly sliced

30 g leek or spring onions (scallions), sliced

20 g celery leaves, sliced

2 Tbsp finely sliced lemon basil (*kemangi*)

2 Tbsp fried shallots

salt, to taste

1. Marinate chicken and prawns with respective spice blends.

2. In separate frying pans, quickly stir-fry chicken and prawns for only 1 minute in very hot oil. Set aside and keep warm.

3. Heat 4 Tbsp oil in a wok or large frying pan (preferably non-stick). Add cabbage and chillies and fry over high heat for 1 minute. Add chilli and soy sauce and fry until almost all the liquid has evaporated.

4. Add shiitake mushrooms and fry for 1 more minute. Add eggs and continue to fry until eggs are scrambled and almost cooked. Add rice, mix well and fry for 1 minute. Add noodles, mix well and fry again for 2 more minutes over high heat. Add spinach, leek, celery and lemon basil, mix well and fry 1 more minute while continuously mixing.

5. Add fried shallots and season to taste with salt.

Rice Cakes Steamed in Banana Leaf *(Ketipat)* *Bali*

Why make rice cakes, *ketipats*?

For one thing, rice cooked in palm leaves is always softer than steamed or boiled rice. Secondly, they are easy to carry. This is the standard means by which cooked rice is carried by a farmer to his field for a snack, or hauled around by the many food pushcarts in Indonesia and by those *warungs* that do not wish to cook rice on the spot. Thirdly, the rice in a *ketipat* can be somewhat overcooked so that it is easier for the older people to chew and digest. Despite being overcooked, rice cooked in a *ketipat* remains soft and not porridge-like. Perhaps this has to do with the confined space in which the rice is cooked.

300 g glutinous rice
50 g shallots, peeled and sliced
20 g garlic, peeled and sliced
10 g galangal (*laos*), peeled and sliced
20 g ginger, peeled and sliced
3 Tbsp vegetable oil
1 stalk lemongrass, bruised
2 kaffir lime leaves
600 ml coconut milk
1 pinch salt

1. Wash rice thoroughly under running water, then drain.

2. Combine shallots, garlic, galangal and ginger in a stone mortar or food processor and grind to a fine paste.

3. Heat oil in a heavy saucepan. Add the paste, lemongrass and kaffir lime leaves and sauté over medium heat for 2 minutes or until fragrant. Add rice and continue to sauté until rice is evenly coated.

4. Fill the saucepan with coconut milk. Add salt, mix well, and bring to a boil. Reduce heat and simmer while continuously stirring until almost all the liquid is absorbed and the rice starts to dry up. Set aside and cool to room temperature.

5. Place 1 heaped Tbsp rice in the centre of a banana leaf and roll up the banana leaf very tightly. Fasten with a bamboo skewer or toothpick and roll up very tightly with a butcher string.

6. Steam for 30 minutes. Cool.

NOTE
If banana leaves are not available, replace with a plastic wrap or even aluminium foil. For a lighter version, replace coconut milk with chicken or vegetable stock.

Jackfruit and Rice Cakes in Coconut Dressing

(Lontong Sayur) Maluku

2 stalks lemongrass, bruised

4 kaffir lime leaves, bruised

500 ml vegetable or chicken stock
(optional) (page 47 or 44)

250 ml coconut cream

300 g young jackfruits, peeled and
sliced into 1 x 2-cm squares

salt, to taste

ground white pepper, to taste

4 chicken eggs, poached

300 g rice cakes (see page 173)

2 Tbsp *sambal* tomato (pages 58-65
to select your favourite)

2 Tbsp fried shallots

SPICE PASTE

3 Tbsp coconut oil

30 g garlic, peeled and sliced

40 g shallots, peeled and finely sliced

30 g ginger, peeled and finely sliced

30 g turmeric, peeled and finely sliced

50 g large red chillies, halved, seeded
and sliced

3-5 bird's eye chillies, finely sliced

50 g peanuts, skin removed and
lightly roasted

1/4 tsp crushed white pepper

1/4 tsp crushed coriander seeds

1. To make the spice paste, combine all ingredients in a stone mortar or food processor and grind into a fine paste.

2. Transfer ground spices into a saucepan. Add lemongrass and kaffir lime leaves and sauté for 2 minutes over medium heat until fragrant.

3. Fill the saucepan with chicken stock and coconut cream and bring to a simmer.

4. Add the young jackfruits and simmer over low heat until the jackfruits are soft. Season broth with salt and ground white pepper to taste.

5. To poach the eggs, heat 1 litre of water to 80°C. Carefully break open only the freshest eggs and place into a strainer to get rid of any water in the egg.

6. With a spoon, stir the water in a circular motion. Slide each egg into a cup and from there into the simmering water. Poach for 5–7 minutes. The egg white needs to be poached slightly and the egg yolk slightly runny. Using a skimmer, take out the eggs and allow the water to run off.

7. Place the cubed rice cakes into the centre of a soup plate and cover with jackfruit soup. Place the poached egg on top and garnish with fried shallots.

8. Serve with your favourite sambal.

NOTE

This is the perfect breakfast dish: tasty, rich in nutrients and good for energy. Many places in Ternate that serve this dish for breakfast are always packed with hungry costumers. Enhance the flavour and taste of this great dish with a grilled fish fillet or even some freshly grilled prawns.

SWEETS
& DESSERTS

Almond Custard *(Srikaya)* *Maluku*

This recipe calls for the use of an oven or steamer. Ovens are rare in Maluku and simple steamers are usually used. Rest a steamer insert on top of a pot of boiling water. Cocottes can be covered with banana leaves or foil.

400 ml coconut milk

250 ml coconut cream

1 or 2 vanilla bean, cut in half and seeds removed into the coconut milk

1 pandan leaf, bruised and squashed

100 g almond slivers

250 ml eggs

100 g castor sugar + extra for sprinkling and caramelising

1 pinch salt

(Refer to page 178, right.)

1. Bring coconut milk and cream, vanilla bean, vanilla core, pandan leaf and almond slivers to a boil. Simmer for 2 minutes. Remove vanilla bean and pandan leaf, completely squeezing out any liquid from the leaf.

2. Mix eggs, sugar and salt till creamy or foamy.

3. Add hot milk to the egg mixture while constantly stirring. Mix well.

4. Pour mixture into individual cocottes.

5. Poach in an 80°C warm water bath in the oven or poach in a steamer at 140°C for approximately 20–30 minutes.

6. Allow to cool. Sprinkle the custard tops with castor sugar and caramelise with a blowtorch.

Baked Coconut Cakes *(Berohcong)* *South Sulawesi*

150 g freshly grated coconut

150 g flour

100 g sugar

3 eggs, beaten

250 ml coconut milk

3 drops vanilla essence

1 pinch salt, to taste

4 Tbsp vegetable oil

(Refer to page 178, left.)

1. Combine all ingredients and whisk into a smooth batter that has the consistency of a relatively thick pancake mix.

2. Preheat muffin tray in an oven at 200°C.

3. Fill each cup with one-quarter cup of batter and bake for 10 minutes, turning the cakes over after 5 minutes or when they turn lightly golden.

NOTE

Berohcong is street food at its very best. Vendors push around carts from one busy area to the next. Of course, ovens would not fit on these street carts; instead they keep a small wood fire going that heats a backing tray. It is this wood fire that imparts a delicious smoky flavour to this cake, which is lightly crispy on the outside but has a rich creamy texture inside. If you wish to add a little of this smoky flavour then simply smoke them as described on page 33 for 10 minutes.

Steamed Corn and Coconut Cakes *(Lenco) Flores*

500 g corn kernels, cleaned, washed, dried and roughly ground

250 g freshly grated coconut

150 g rice flour

100 g castor sugar

1 tsp salt

corn husks, as needed for wrapping

bamboo skewers, as needed

bamboo strings, as needed

1. Combine corn kernels, grated coconut, rice flour, sugar and salt. Mix into a smooth dough.

2. Cut corn husks into even squares. Place 2 heaped Tbsp corn mixture into the centre of a corn husk square. Fold into a tight parcel and fasten with bamboo skewers. Repeat with remaining ingredients. Secure parcels tightly with bamboo strings.

3. Steam parcels for 15 minutes.

Steamed Cassava Cake *(Songkol)* *Flores*

This delicious cake has a texture similar to bread and is best served after a meal with a piping hot cup of coffee. Traditionally, cassava cakes are steamed in bamboo tubes, which impart a very unique flavour.

500 g cassava flour
125 g freshly grated coconut
100 ml coconut cream
100 g palm sugar, finely chopped
1 pinch salt
125 ml water
banana leaves, as needed
biscuit tins, soufflé cups or 7-cm cake rings can be used as moulds

1. Combine cassava flour with grated coconut, coconut cream, palm sugar and salt and mix well.

2. Gradually add water and continue to mix until a soft, lump-free mixture is achieved. Set aside.

3. Scald the banana leaves in boiling water or over an open flame. Line small moulds with the softened banana leaves and fill loosely with cassava mix. Cover moulds with banana leaves.

4. Steam for 30 minutes. Serve warm.

Rice Flour Dumplings in Palm Sugar Sauce

(*Jaja Batun Bedil*) *Bali*

In Bali, we serve this Indonesian-style gnocchi, quenelles or spaetzle with lots of coconut cream. However, vanilla or cinnamon ice cream will complement this dish as well. Alternatively, blend two-thirds coconut cream with one-third dairy whipping cream and pressurise the mixture to get whipped coconut cream.

DUMPLINGS

150 g glutinous rice flour

50 g tapioca flour

1 pinch salt

160 ml water (Depending on the flour and water quality, you might have to add a little more or a little less water. Add the given amount of water first and then add the rest gradually, tablespoon by tablespoon.)

PALM SUGAR SYRUP

125 ml water

125 g palm sugar, chopped

1 pandan leaf, bruised

1 pinch salt

(Refer to page 183, right.)

1. To make the dumplings, place rice flour, tapioca flour and salt into a deep mixing bowl. Gradually add water and mix well. Knead into a smooth dough. The dough must not be too dry but soft and elastic, almost runny.

2. To prepare the syrup, combine all ingredients in a saucepan. Bring to a boil and simmer for 5 minutes.

3. Roll small dumplings into approximately 1 cm in diameter, which you directly drop into the simmering palm sugar syrup. This process should only take about 5 minutes until all the dough is used up. Once all the dumplings are in the syrup, continue to simmer for 5 more minutes. The starch of the dumplings will thicken the syrup to the right consistency.

4. Allow dumplings to cool to room temperature in syrup.

Steamed Pumpkin Cake (*Empek Ndesi*) *Flores*

500 g pumpkin, peeled and finely shredded

250 g freshly grated coconut

150 g rice flour

100 g crystal sugar

1 pinch salt

banana leaves for wrapping

(Refer to page 183, left.)

1. Combine pumpkin, coconut, rice flour, sugar and salt. Mix well into a smooth dough.

2. Cut banana leaves into 18 x 22-cm rectangular squares. Steam the leaves for 10 seconds, or place for 5 seconds over an open gas flame, or microwave for 3 seconds. This will soften the leaf fibres and make the banana leaves pliable.

3. Place 2 heaped Tbsp pumpkin filling on the centre of each banana leaf. Fold one-third of the banana leaf over the filling and roll up tightly. Secure the ends with skewers or toothpicks.

4. Steam parcels for 15 minutes.

5. Serve warm, laced with coconut cream.

NOTE
This cake is delicious when served with a rich, creamy ice cream.

Black Rice Pudding *(Bubuh Injin)* Bali

Bubuh injin translates into "black rice porridge", which is actually misleading as the final dish must have the consistency of a risotto. The dish should look very black and be like a porridge, but the grain of the rice must still be slightly "al dente" with a touch of bite to it. If pandan is difficult to find, then replace with cinnamon or even a vanilla bean.

250 g black glutinous rice

50 g white glutinous rice

2 pandan leaves, torn

800 ml water (optional: a very light coconut milk)

100-125g palm sugar, chopped to taste

1 pinch salt, to taste

125 ml coconut cream

(Refer to pages 182-183, centre.)

1. Rinse both black and white glutinous rice well for 2 minutes under running water. Drain. Soak in water for 8 hours. Drain.

2. Place water, both black and white glutinous rice and pandan leaves into pressure cooker. Quickly bring to a boil.

3. Pressure cook at 1 bar / 15 psi for 15 minutes (see pages 21-22). Turn off heat and allow to cool for 30 minutes before opening pressure cooker.

4. Add palm sugar and continue to simmer until a smooth, slightly runny consistency similar to a risotto is achieved. Season with a pinch of salt. Remove from heat and allow to cool to room temperature.

5. When serving, top with a generous amount of coconut cream.

HELPFUL HINTS
As fresh coconut milk turns rancid fairly quickly, a pinch of salt is usually added to the milk to help preserve it for a few hours. A more effective alternative is to cook the coconut milk with 1 tsp cornstarch diluted in a little water; heat gently and stir constantly for a couple of minutes. This coconut sauce will keep overnight. Milk made from instant powdered coconut will not turn rancid, although the flavour is not as good as fresh coconut milk.

Cassava Dumplings in Palm Sugar Sauce

(Kolak Bola Bola) *Flores*

Cassava adapts and grows easily in almost any soil, even in extremely dry conditions. Because of this it is often used as a substitute crop for rice. Cassava is grown in every backyard and eaten almost daily in every home. It is extremely versatile, and contains very high amounts of nutrients.

600 g cassava, peeled and finely grated
100 g white sugar
3 Tbsp coconut cream
1 pinch salt

SAUCE
2 cups coconut milk
100 g palm sugar
1 pinch salt

1. To prepare the sauce, combine coconut milk, palm sugar and salt in a saucepan and bring to a boil over medium heat. Simmer for 2 minutes.

2. To make the dumplings, fold kitchen towel over grated cassava and squeeze out any fluid.

3. Place cassava into a mixing bowl. Add sugar, coconut cream and salt. Knead into a smooth dough.

4. Using the palms of your hands, roll out little round bite-sized dumplings and drop them into the simmering coconut-palm sugar sauce.

5. Poach the dumplings at very low heat for about 10 minutes or until dumplings are soft and tender.

6. Best served warm or at room temperature.

NOTE
A scoop of coconut or vanilla ice cream will make these dumplings simply irresistible.

Roasted Coconut Snack (Rebok) *Flores*

Rebok tastes best as a snack with a glass of coffee or a piping hot cup of tea. This crunchy, tasty snack adds a little bite when sprinkled over whipped cream, crème brulee, ice cream, mousse cakes or simply atop an assortment of freshly sliced fruits.

500 g long grain rice
250 g freshly grated coconut
125 g palm sugar, finely chopped
1 pinch salt

1. Wash and soak rice in water for 30 minutes. Drain.

2. Place rice in a stone mortar or food processor and grind into a medium-fine flour. Sieve through a medium-fine mesh.

3. Combine flour and coconut in a wok and roast over medium heat until golden and very dry. Remove from heat and place mixture into a mixing bowl. Cool.

4. Add palm sugar and mix well until palm sugar is dissolved and blended well with rice-coconut mixture. Season to taste with salt.

NOTE
Store in airtight containers as *rebok* can be kept for several weeks in a dry place.

Coconut Vanilla Cake *(Bika Ambon)* *Sumatra North*

When preparing this cake, you may want to double this recipe as this cake not only tastes terrific when freshly baked, but it can also keep for several days when refrigerated. Coffee or tea goes well with a large slice of *bika ambon* warmed in the microwave for a few seconds.

YEAST DOUGH
50 ml coconut water
8 g instant yeast
50 g flour
1 pinch salt

250 ml coconut milk
3 pandan leaves
1 stalk lemongrass, bruised
3 kaffir lime leaves
1 vanilla bean, halved and seeded
2 g salt
6 eggs
4 egg yolks
150 g sugar
2-3 drops yellow food colouring (optional)
135 g tapioca flour, sieved

(Refer to pages 188-189, centre.)

1. In a deep bowl, combine coconut water, yeast, flour and salt and mix well into an elastic dough. Cover with a damp towel and set aside at room temperature for 1 hour.

2. In a saucepan, combine coconut milk, pandan leaves, lemongrass, kaffir lime leaves, vanilla bean and salt. Mix well and bring slowly to a boil. Set aside and cool to room temperature. Strain.

3. In a deep bowl, combine eggs, egg yolks, sugar, flavoured coconut milk and optional food colouring and whisk well. Fold in tapioca flour and blend into a smooth batter that has a rather liquid texture.

4. Add starter yeast and blend into a smooth dough. The consistency will be rather liquid, similar to a pancake mix.

5. Dust a cake pan or muffin moulds with flour and fill evenly with batter.

6. Place in a moderately hot oven at around 160°C for 20–30 minutes until golden brown.

Rice Flour Dumplings filled with Palm Sugar *(Klepon)* *Bali*

Klepon is the perfect condiment at the end of a dinner in place of the usual heavy pralines. One simple way to fill these tasty dumpling is to insert a small piece of hardened palm sugar into the centre.

DOUGH
150 g glutinous rice flour
50 g tapioca flour
1 pinch salt
160 ml warm water (add a little more or less for the right consistency)

FILLING
100 g palm sugar, chopped
2 Tbsp water

175 g freshly grated coconut

(Refer to page 189, right.)

1. Combine glutinous rice flour, tapioca flour and salt and blend well. Add water and knead dough into a smooth, soft, elastic dough.

2. Divide dough into small 8 g balls, using a little rice flour to prevent dough from sticking.

3. To make the filling, combine palm sugar and water in a small saucepan and simmer over low heat and reduce into a syrup. Cool.

4. Use a syringe, inject small amounts of palm sugar syrup into the centre of the balls.

5. Bring 3 litres of lightly salted water to boil. Add dumplings, mix gently to prevent dumplings from sticking and simmer until the dumplings float to the surface.

6. Drain water and plunge dumplings into ice water for 1 second; do not cool them. Drain water and allow dumplings to dry.

7. Roll dumplings individually in grated coconut.

Creamed Mung Beans *(Bubuh Injin)* *Bali*

Creamed mung beans is a favourite breakfast dish throughout Indonesia although I prefer this healthy sweet snack as a dessert. To make the dessert more interesting, top the slightly warm dish with your favourite vanilla-based ice cream.

500 g mung beans, washed and soaked for 8 hours
1 litre light coconut milk
50 g ginger, peeled, sliced and crushed
2 pandan leaves, bruised
150-200 g white sugar
1 pinch salt

TOPPING
½ cup grated coconut
coconut cream, to taste

(Refer to page 188, left.)

1. Winnow the beans to remove the husks and pick out broken beans and impurities.

2. To add flavour, perform this optional step of heating the beans briefly on a hot steel pan without oil. This adds a slightly singed taste, but be careful not to burn them.

3. Place the mung beans, coconut milk, ginger and pandan leaves into a pressure cooker and bring to a boil. Cover.

4. Pressure cook at 1 bar / 15 bar for 7 minutes (see pages 21-22). Turn off heat and allow it to cool for 20 minutes. Open cover and check whether the beans are cooked thoroughly. Sometimes the beans have to be brought back to a simmer to cook them a little more and reduce the liquid.

5. Add sugar and a pinch of salt. Serve with grated coconut and coconut cream.

Fried Bananas with Sweet Chilli Sauce

(Pisang Goreng dan Sambal Tomat Pedas) Maluku

We discovered this unusual combination of fried bananas and sweet chilli sauce on the island of Ternate in a seaside restaurant. The people of Ternate call the sauce *pedas*, which means hot and spicy but this is an overstatement as the sugar and lime juice balances the spiciness perfectly.

FRIED BANANAS

²/₃ cup all-purpose flour

²/₃ cup water

1 pinch salt

8 finger bananas or large bananas, halved

¹/₃ cup rice flour

oil for frying

SWEET CHILLI SAUCE

150 g large chillies

25 g bird's eye chillies

50 g shallots, peeled and cut into halves

200 g tomato, peeled and seeded

¹/₄ tsp dried prawn (shrimp) paste (*terasi*), roasted

25 g palm sugar, chopped

25 g white sugar

50 ml coconut oil

2 Tbsp lime juice

salt, to taste

1. To make the fried bananas, combine flour, water and salt in a deep mixing bowl. Whisk vigorously until the batter is even and smooth and not too thin, and has the consistency of a pancake mix.

2. Dust bananas evenly with rice flour. Dip bananas individually into batter. Make sure the bananas are generously coated with batter.

3. Heat a generous amount of oil in a heavy saucepan to about 120°C.

4. Add bananas and simultaneously increase the temperature of the oil slowly to around 160°C, which should take about 20 minutes. Remove and drain for a minute on a paper towel.

5. To prepare the chilli sauce, grill chillies, shallots and tomatoes until skins are evenly black. Remove seeds and skins of the large chillies and the tomatoes.

6. Place chillies, tomatoes, shallots, shrimp paste, palm sugar, white sugar and coconut oil into a stone mortar or food processor and grind into a coarse, creamy paste.

7. Season to taste with lime juice and salt.

NOTE
Sweet potatoes and jackfruit can be fried in the same way. Most firm fruits make a delightful snack in between meals, especially with a glass of coffee or tea.

Spicy Sweet and Sour Mangoes

(*Rujak Manga*) *Flores*

One of the most popular snacks in Indonesia is *rujak* – a mixture of crisp, unripe, sliced fruits served uncooked with sweet and sour sauce. Unripe fruits of some local trees and fruits of inferior taste can be converted into a very popular snack dish called *rujak* and *petis*. Although these fruit snacks are almost always available from pushcart paddlers in the village, people like to make them. It is best to use crisp or unripe fruits to give the dish its proper texture. Unripe mangoes are a favourite. Using them in *rujak* allows the taste to be tempered by the spicy sauce that covers the fruit. Some fruits like water apple and guava are naturally crisp when ripe. The tuber *bangkuan*, similar to *jicama* (yam bean) is also properly used, as are cucumbers, unripe papaya and others.

3-5 bird's eye chillies, finely sliced
3 Tbsp palm sugar
2 Tbsp tamarind water (see page 69)
2 Tbsp lime juice
1 pinch salt, to taste
400 g green mangoes, sliced
1 Tbsp chopped and roasted peanuts

1. To make the sauce, combine all ingredients except the mangoes and the tamarind water in a heavy stone mortar or food processor and grind into a very fine paste.

2. Gradually add the tamarind water and blend the mix into a smooth creamy sauce.

3. Combine sliced mangoes and sauce and blend well. Season to taste with a pinch of salt.

4. Garnish with roasted peanuts.

Creamed Egg Tea *(Teh Telur)* West Sumatra

Instead of a hot chocolate, try this delicious tea that will thoroughly warm you up in cold weather and give you energy at the same time. This typical breakfast drink is widely served on the west coast of Sumatra in place of coffee.

4 egg yolks
4 Tbsp sugar
600 ml hot black tea
lime wedges (optional)

1. In a food processor, combine egg yolks and sugar and whisk at medium speed into a foamy cream.

2. Divide the cream equally into four warmed glasses.

3. Fill up the glasses with hot tea and mix well.

4. Optional: Serve with lime wedges.

INDONESIAN SPICES

Black nut

Candlenut

Cardamom

Large red chillies

Small chillies

Black nut – *Keluak*
The fruit of this tropical tree has a hard, black-grey shell similar in shape to a mussel. Tucked inside is a black nut with a very delicate texture. The shell should not be opened until needed in order to preserve the moisture and delicate texture of the nut. To prepare the nut, soak it in boiling water until soft. The spicy brown mass is then blended with other spices and flavourings, imparting a delicious aroma to any recipe. It is available outside Indonesia in a shelled form in oriental food markets.

Candlenut – *Kemiri*
The candlenut seed is an indispensable spice in Indonesian cuisine. Possessing little flavour on its own, its main role is as a thickener. The seeds should not be eaten raw as they are poisonous and have a laxative effect. When shelled, the round, creamy, brittle, waxy yellowish nut that is similar only in appearance to the macadamia nut is also used as a binding agent for sauces, adding a faint flavour to dishes. If unavailable, substitute with raw peanuts without the shells and skin or raw cashews.

Cardamom – *Kapulaga*
Cardamom grows wild in gaps in the evergreen monsoon forests of the Western Ghates in Southern India and the Western highlands of Sri Lanka. The strong, almost eucalyptus-like flavour of cardamom can be tasted mainly in Indonesia's lamb dishes. The whitish, fibrous pod encloses pungent black seeds, which release a very strong perfumed aroma when finely crushed in a stone mortar. The taste is lemony and flowery, with a note of camphor or eucalyptus. It is mainly used in Sumatra where the spice was introduced by early visitors from the Middle East.

Chillies – *Cabe*
Capsicum peppers were introduced to Asia in the 16th century by Portuguese and Spanish explorers via trade routes from South America. Today, capsicum peppers are the most widely-used condiment in the world. Its fruits are eaten as a vegetable or used as a spice and they are consumed fresh, or in dried or processed forms. Indonesians love chillies in their food and often use what would be considered an excessive amount by Western standards. Chillies grown in Indonesia come in many colours, shapes and sizes. They can be as tiny as a small baby's finger or as long as 20 centimetres. When buying chillies, make sure they are very firm to the touch, shiny and smooth-skinned, and the stems are green and crunchy. It is best to use chillies immediately. Avoid storing them for extended periods in the refrigerator, which will intensify their spiciness and change their natural crisp clean flavour and aroma. The Indonesian cook mostly uses three types of chillies with the level of spiciness increasing inversely as the size of the chilli gets smaller. Always wear gloves when handling chillies and wash your hands and all surfaces that have come into contact with them. Contrary to common belief, it is not the seeds that are spicy but the "placenta" or membrane that connects the seed with the chilli. When the seeds are used, a bitter taste infuses the dish.

Large red chillies – *Lombok*
By far the mildest chillies found in Indonesia, they are mainly used as flavouring because they have little or no bite. These finger-sized chillies are always seeded before use. If using spicy chillies, the quantity should be reduced by one-third or even by half.

Small chillies – *Tabia*
These short fat chillies are about 2.5-cm long and are the preferred chilli of choice for most Indonesian dishes. They are normally chopped or bruised, adding a genuine kick to dishes.

Bird's eye chillies – *Tabia rawit*
These tiny chillies are extremely spicy. They are mostly used raw and served as a condiment.

Cinnamon – *Kayu manis*
This delicately fragrant, slightly sweet spice has 150-250 species occurring in continental Asia, Malaysia,

Bird's eye chillies   Cinnamon   Clove

Australia, the Pacific, and a few species found in Central and South America. Cassia and cinnamon are among the oldest of spices, reportedly reaching ancient Egypt by the 17th century BC. Cinnamon is the dried bark of an evergreen tree whose inner bark is cut and peeled from the new growth of the trees, curling to form the familiar long "quills" or sticks. Most of the cinnamon sold in Indonesia is from the bark of the species *brumanni*, (*cinnamomum burmanni*) found in Sumatra. Avoid using ground cinnamon and opt for the bark instead, which adds a much softer flavour to dishes. Cinnamon with its pleasant, sweet woody aroma is delicate yet intense; the taste is fragrant and warm with a hint of clove and citrus. When chewed fresh, the bark releases a pleasant spicy sweet flavour.

Clove – *Cengkeh*

The clove tree was first cultivated on Ternate in the Moluccan islands of Indonesia and it grows wild there as it does in New Guinea. The clove crop and its trade have a long and fascinating history dating back to the Han Dynasty in the 3rd century BC. The story of the clove trade and the spread of the crop is one of intrigue and brutality. Apart from pepper, no other spice may have played a comparable role in world history. Early in the 17th century when the Dutch ousted the Portuguese from the Moluccas, clove cultivation had spread to many islands. Under Dutch rule, the crop was forcibly eradicated and its cultivation concentrated in Ambon and three nearby islands. From the Moluccas the clove tree was taken to other parts of Asia. Early in the 19th century the British took plants to Malaysia, Sumatra, India and Sri Lanka. During various expeditions in the 17th century, the French appropriated cuttings from trees that escaped the Dutch axe and took them from the North Moluccas to Mauritius. These plants gave rise to the clove population now found outside Asia, in Zanzibar, Madagascar, and most recently in Brazil at Bahia. The clove tree is a member of the myrtle family and native to Southeast Asia, growing up to 9 metres tall and flourishing only in tropical climates at higher elevations. Many Indonesian mountain ranges are covered in this very pretty,

reddish-looking tree whose unopened flower bud encloses this precious spice. After harvesting, cloves are dried until they turn a reddish-brown colour and become full-flavoured. Indonesia is the largest producer and consumer of cloves on the planet and yet cloves are very seldom used in cooking; instead, they are mainly used to flavour tobacco, which is rolled into Indonesia's notorious clove cigarettes, the *kretek*. The aroma of cloves is assertive and warm, with notes of pepper and camphor. The taste is fruity but also sharp, hot and bitter, imparting a numbing sensation in the mouth.

Coconut cream – *Santan*

People generally use coconut cream in curries, desserts and cakes because it enhances the aromas and tastes of the dishes and you can obtain it easily and cheaply from your nearby supermarket or grocery store. Coconut cream also contains good saturated fats that are beneficial to your health and it aids weight loss as it is easily converted to energy once your body absorbs it. In other words, it does not transform into bad cholesterol that clogs up your arteries and triggers heart problems and stroke. Most importantly, it does not cause easy weight gain. Its lauric acid content (which scientists and researchers have found in human breast milk) also helps the human body to fight viruses and bacteria, and promotes normal brain development and healthy bones. Its anti-carcinogenic and anti-pathogenic properties can also help keep cancer at bay.

Coconut oil – *Minyak kelapa*

While coconut possesses many health benefits due to its fibre and nutritional content, its oil makes it a truly remarkable food and medicine. Once mistakenly believed to be unhealthy because of its high saturated fat content, it is now known that the fat in coconut oil is unique and different from other fats and possesses many health-promoting properties. Coconut oil has been described as "the healthiest oil on earth".

Coriander seeds

Cumin

Galangal

Lesser galangal

Garlic

Coriander seeds – *Ketumbar*

Coriander is a commonly used spice in Indonesian cooking, which mostly uses the dry seeds that are often roasted before being thoroughly crushed. No different from the spice that is used in the West under the same name, coriander is delicate yet complex, with a suggestion of pepper, mint, and lemon. Coriander seeds are among only a handful of dry spices that are used in Indonesian cooking.

Cumin – *Cintan putih*

Originally cultivated in Iran and the Mediterranean, cumin is mentioned in both the Old and New Testaments of the Bible and was a table condiment in Greece and North Africa. Cumin fruits were highly prized in ancient civilisations as one of the most aromatic of all culinary spices. In Indonesia, cumin has been cultivated for centuries in higher mountainous regions and is a popular spice in many dishes. Because of its strong flavour, only small quantities are needed to impact the taste of a dish. The smell of cumin is strong and heavy, spicy sweet, with acrid but warm depth. The flavour is rich, slightly bitter, sharp, earthy and warm with a persistent pungency.

Galangal – *Laos, lengkuas*

The exact origin of galangal is unknown; the earliest reports of its use come from south China and Java. Today galangal is cultivated in all of Southeast Asia. The tough but delicately scented rhizome stem must be peeled and sliced before use. When purchased fresh, wash galangal thoroughly, then wrap with a damp cloth before placing it into an airtight container or bag. Place the container or bag into the refrigerator - this allows galangal to stay fresh for up to two weeks.

Lesser galangal – *Kencur*

Botanically a member of the ginger family, this ingredient is subject to some confusion caused by the many names by which it is known. The Balinese call it "cekuh"; for the sake of simplicity we refer to it by its Indonesian name of "kencur". *Kencur* is a delicate root with thin brown skin, lemon-coloured crisp flesh, with a unique, very strong, camphor-like, musky, peppery, earthy taste somewhat similar to young ginger and galangal. It has strong, overpowering aroma and must be used sparingly. Of all the spices used in Indonesian cooking, this is one of the most difficult to find in the West. If unavailable, replace a given quantity in a recipe with ½ ginger and ½ galangal.

Garlic – *Bawang putih*

Garlic is believed to have originated from central Asia (Tien Shan) where its wild ancestor is endemic. Garlic spread to the Mediterranean region in ancient times, and was already known in Egypt in 3000 BC. It is also an ancient crop in India. The Spanish, Portuguese, and French introduced it to the New World. In Indonesia, garlic resembles Western garlic but with cloves that are generally smaller, a smell that is a lot less pungent and a flavour that is less sharp than the European or the bleached Chinese varieties. Garlic is without doubt one of the most popular ingredients in Indonesian cooking; there is hardly an Indonesian dish without this ingredient. Try to purchase young, unbruised garlic with firm heads at the beginning of the growing season as they are much softer and milder in flavour. To peel garlic easily, crush each clove lightly with the flat blade of a heavy knife or cleaver.

Ginger – *Jahe*

Ginger has been grown in tropical Asia since ancient times. Wild forms of ginger are unknown and its origin is uncertain. Many believe ginger was originally from India and was brought to Europe and East Africa by Arab traders from India. Together with pepper, ginger was one of the most commonly traded spices during the 13th-14th centuries. From East Africa, the Portuguese brought ginger to West Africa and other regions of the tropics in the 16th century. At about the same period, the Spanish introduced ginger into Jamaica, which still produces high quality ginger. Today ginger is cultivated throughout the humid tropics. The underground rhizome of an attractive flowering plant, ginger is widely used in Indonesian cooking. The rhizome stem should be plump and firm, and must always be peeled, after which it is then either sliced or pounded.

Ginger

Lemon basil

Lemongrass

Long pepper

Nutmeg

Ginger is easily available in most Asian stores or supermarkets and recipes calling for ginger should never be substituted with powdered ginger. Whenever possible, only use very young ginger.

Lemon basil – *Don kemangi*

Sweet basil is known to have been cultivated in India for 5,000 years. Today it occurs naturally or in naturalised forms throughout the tropics, subtropics and warm temperate areas. Records of its cultivation were found in Egypt 3,000 years ago and it most probably made its way from there to the Middle East, Greece, Italy, and the rest of Europe. This delicate spice has a very pleasant lemon-basil flavour used mostly in fish dishes, which are wrapped in banana leaves before cooking. If used in cooked dishes, then finely sliced lemon basil should be added near the end of the cooking process to retain its clean, lemony fragrance. Regular basil or Thai basil can be used as a substitute for lemon basil.

Lemongrass – *Serai*

The exact origins of lemongrass are not known, but Malaysia is most likely its birthplace. Lemongrass is a cultivated plant found throughout South and Southeast Asia. Today it is grown in tropical areas around the globe. Lemongrass grows easily in most soils where sunshine and water are abundant. In Bali and the islands to the east, almost every home has lemongrass growing in its yard. The flavour of lemongrass is refreshingly tart, clean and citrus-like. When buying the stalks, check that they are smooth and firm, not wrinkled or dry. Fresh lemongrass will keep for 2-3 weeks in the refrigerator if wrapped in plastic. Peel off the harder outer parts, which can be used for stocks and sauces. The softer inner parts should be lightly bruised before use, or bruised and very finely sliced. When used as an ingredient in a spice paste or sauce, bruise the lemongrass along the whole length and tie into a knot. This will prevent the lemongrass fibres from falling apart. If lemongrass is unavailable, substitute with lemon or ideally, lime zests, which should be added to the dish at the end of the cooking process.

Long pepper – *Cabai panjang, Cabe java*

There are more than 1,200 species of pepper, most occurring in tropical regions. Over 400 species have been recorded in the Malaysian region alone. Most pepper species originate from South and Southeast Asia. Long pepper grows wild in Thailand, Indo-China, Malaysia and the Philippines to the Moluccas and throughout Indonesia. The spikes of the fruit are harvested green and sundried. Long pepper is usually used whole. It smells sweetly fragrant, and initially resembles black pepper in taste, but it has a biting, numbing aftertaste. Long pepper is also widely applied medicinally throughout Indonesia as a tonic for a variety of digestive and intestinal disorders. If long pepper is not available, it can be replaced with black pepper.

Nutmeg – *Pala*

Inside the apricot-like fruit lies a hard seed, the kernel of which is the nutmeg. Around this seed is a lace covering or aril - the by-product of mace. Nutmeg has a rich, fresh and highly aromatic flavour with a hint of clove. Nutmeg is best bought whole and will keep in airtight containers for a long time. Avoid using powdered nutmeg as the powerful flavour is quickly lost. Always grate whole nutmegs. This most aromatic sweet spice is often used with strongly flavoured meats such as pork, duck and lamb.

Palm sugar – *Gula merah or gula java*

Among sugar-producing trees, certain tropical palms rank among the most bountiful in their potential harvest. The sugar and lontar palm or the coconut tree can be tapped for up to half the year, yielding 4-6 litres per day. Individual trees can produce between 5-40 kg of sugar per year. The sap is collected from the flowering stalks at the top of the tree, or from taps in the trunk, and then boiled down to a thick syrupy mass which is then poured into halved coconut shells or bamboo stems where it is cooled and set to be sold in cylindrical or round cakes.

Palm sugar

Pandan leaf

Peanuts

White Pepper

Black Pepper

Pandan leaf (screwpine) – *Don pandan*

Cultigens or fragrant pandan now exists only in its cultivated form. Its cultivation is widespread throughout Asia, playing a significant role in the everyday ceremonial life of the Balinese. Large pandan leaves are finely shredded and then placed on religious offerings, releasing a wonderfully sweet scent. Pandan leaves are very aromatic, with a sweet, fresh, floral and lightly musky odour. Leaves must be strongly bruised before use to release their flavour. Purchase only crisp, smooth, strong, green-coloured leaves, which you can keep in the refrigerator for 2-3 weeks in a plastic container. Pandan leaves have a wide variety of uses ranging from enhancing curries to flavouring rice dishes such as Indonesia's famous yellow rice (*nasi kuning*).

Peanuts – *Kacang tanah*

Peanuts originate from an area in southern Bolivia and Northwest Argentina in South America. The Portuguese took them from Brazil to West Africa and then to Southwestern India in the 16th century. At the same time, the Spaniards introduced them from Mexico to the Western Pacific, from where they subsequently spread to China, Indonesia and to Madagascar. Peanuts are easy to grow and require little water, explaining their widespread presence in many dry coastal regions in Indonesia. Popular as a snack, they are often steamed, which produces a softer but still crunchy nut. Roasted, peeled peanuts are usually called *kacang asin*. Fried peeled peanuts are called *kacang kapri*. Shelled raw peanuts with their skin still intact are normally used to make Indonesia's famous blended peanut sauce, widely served blended with vegetables (*gado gado* in Indonesia, *pecelan* in Bali) or as a condiment with *satays* – grilled meat skewers. When choosing raw peanuts, look for those with the skins still on. Peanuts are tastier and more flavoursome when they are deep-fried or roasted in the skin. If not available raw, substitute with peanuts that have been roasted in their shells. These are available in most supermarkets.

Pepper – *Merica / lada*

Pepper is native to Western Ghats of Kerala State, India, where it occurs wild in the mountains. Pepper reached Southeast Asia as early as 100 BC, brought by Hindus migrating from India to Indonesia and other countries in the region. The use of dried pepper as a food flavouring was already known in classical Rome and Europe, where it was highly valued as an import as early as the 12th century. Despite the long history of pepper in the region, there is no tradition of consuming black and white pepper in Indonesia. In recent years, however, its use as a spice in food flavouring and preservation has gradually increased due to expanding tourism development. Indonesians prefer *tabia bun–long* pepper as a standard ingredient in their cooking. Black and white pepper come from the same plant, a woody climber that can reach a height of 10 metres or more. The spice derives from the berry-like fruit of the plant. These are dried and sold as black pepper. Alternatively, they may be stripped of their outer hulls, either mechanically or by fermentation, producing the milder white pepper. Indonesia is the second largest producer of pepper in the world after Brazil. In Indonesian markets, black pepper is always sold as whole peppercorns and never ground. Black pepper has a fine, fruity pungent fragrance with a warm, woody note, and a hot biting taste. While white pepper is less aromatic, it has a sharp pungency. Pepper loses its aroma and flavour when ground, so it is best to buy whole berries and grind in a pepper mill or crush in a mortar as needed.

Prawn (shrimp) paste – *Terasi*

Made by drying prawns under the sun and then pounding them into a pulp, this pungent paste is available in small packages in all markets across Indonesia. Grilled or roasted without oil before using, this is done to neutralise its strong fishy flavour. Roasted prawn paste can be stored for several months in airtight containers. Although pungent, prawn paste adds a pleasant flavour when used in dishes.

Prawn (shrimp) paste

Salam leaf

Shallots

Turmeric

Turmeric water

Salam leaf – *Don salam*
This aromatic leaf is widely distributed throughout Myanmar, Indo-China, Thailand, Malaysia and Indonesia. In Indonesia it is mainly used dried as a spice to flavour soups, meat, chicken, fish and vegetable dishes. The leaves are added early in the cooking process and are left to cook with the dish as the flavour develops only gradually. Although similar to the bay leaf in use and appearance, they are completely different and should not be used as a substitute for each other. The leaves are sold in bundles in markets throughout Indonesia, and many families grow them in their backyard for home use. If the salam leaf is unavailable, replace it with dry or even fresh kaffir lime leaves.

Shallots – *Bawang merah*
The "bawang merah kecil" or shallot traces its ancestry to France where it was first cultivated in the 12th century. Widespread domestication followed in Tadzhikstan, Afghanistan and Iran. A relative of the onion, these shallots are an essential ingredient in many Indonesian dishes and should not be confused with green spring onions that are sometimes also called "shallots". The shallots found in Indonesia are normally rather small and it will require patience to peel and clean the enormous amounts required in everyday cooking. Shallots are peeled and then sliced or ground, used as a garnish and flavouring or thinly sliced and deep-fried. Packets of thinly sliced deep-fried shallots are available in Asian grocery stores. Indonesian shallots are very similar in appearance to the shallots sold in the West but they are usually smaller and subtler in flavour. If shallots are not available, substitute with red Spanish onions.

Shallot leaves – *Don bawang merah*
The leaves of the shallots resemble spring onions or green onions. Finely sliced, they are often added to vegetable dishes and salad-like dishes. They taste terrific as flavouring in stocks.

Soy sauce – *Kecap asin & kecap manis*
Soy sauce originated in China and became a kitchen staple all across Asia. It is a sauce made from the fermentation of soybeans, roasted grain, water and salt. A popular brand found throughout the world in many Asian stores is ABC.

Turmeric – *Kunyit*
Often misspelled and mispronounced as "tumeric", this herbaceous plant is thought to have originated from India. Turmeric now grows in a naturalised state in the teak forests of East Java. Turmeric is also good for health; it is believed that a high consumption of the spice prevents the onset of Alzheimer's disease. India is the centre of domestication for turmeric where it has been grown since time immemorial. Turmeric reached China before the 7th century, East Africa in the 8th century and West Africa in the 13th century. Today it is widely cultivated throughout the tropics, but cultivation on a large scale is largely confined to India and Southeast Asia. The primary use of turmeric rhizome stems is as a culinary spice, constituting 20-25% of the ingredient in curry powder. An attractive perennial with large lily-like leaves and yellow flowers, turmeric is a member of the ginger family and, like ginger, the underground rhizome stem of the plant is used in cooking. The brownish skin must be scraped or peeled to expose its bright yellow flesh. Fresh turmeric is crunchy with a rich, gingery, citrus aroma and a pleasant earthy flavour. Fresh turmeric adds a wonderful flavour and a rich golden-yellow hue to dishes. If fresh turmeric is not available, substitute with 1½ Tbsp turmeric powder per 100 g fresh, peeled roots. In many parts of Indonesia, finely sliced turmeric leaves are used as seasoning in many dishes.

Turmeric water – *Air kunyit*
Combine an equal amount of peeled and finely chopped turmeric with the same amount of warm water and grind in a stone mortar or food processor until very fine; strain through a fine sieve or kitchen mousseline cloth.

WEIGHTS & MEASURES

Quantities for this book are given in Metric, Imperial and American (spoon) measures. Standard spoon and cup measurements used are: 1 tsp = 5 ml, 1 Tbsp = 15 ml, 1 cup = 250 ml. All measures are level unless otherwise stated.

LIQUID AND VOLUME MEASURES

Metric	Imperial	American
5 ml	$^1/_6$ fl oz	1 teaspoon
10 ml	$^1/_3$ fl oz	1 dessertspoon
15 ml	$^1/_2$ fl oz	1 tablespoon
60 ml	2 fl oz	$^1/_4$ cup (4 tablespoons)
85 ml	$2^1/_2$ fl oz	$^1/_3$ cup
90 ml	3 fl oz	$^3/_8$ cup (6 tablespoons)
125 ml	4 fl oz	$^1/_2$ cup
180 ml	6 fl oz	$^3/_4$ cup
250 ml	8 fl oz	1 cup
300 ml	10 fl oz ($^1/_2$ pint)	$1^1/_4$ cups
375 ml	12 fl oz	$1^1/_2$ cups
435 ml	14 fl oz	$1^3/_4$ cups
500 ml	16 fl oz	2 cups
625 ml	20 fl oz (1 pint)	$2^1/_2$ cups
750 ml	24 fl oz ($1^1/_5$ pints)	3 cups
1 litre	32 fl oz ($1^3/_5$ pints)	4 cups
1.25 litres	40 fl oz (2 pints)	5 cups
1.5 litres	48 fl oz ($2^2/_5$ pints)	6 cups
2.5 litres	80 fl oz (4 pints)	10 cups

OVEN TEMPERATURE

	°C	°F	Gas Regulo
Very slow	120	250	1
Slow	150	300	2
Moderately slow	160	325	3
Moderate	180	350	4
Moderately hot	190/200	370/400	5/6
Hot	210/220	410/440	6/7
Very hot	230	450	8
Super hot	250/290	475/550	9/10

LENGTH

Metric	Imperial
0.5 cm	$^1/_4$ inch
1 cm	$^1/_2$ inch
1.5 cm	$^3/_4$ inch
2.5 cm	1 inch

DRY MEASURES

Metric	Imperial
30 grams	1 ounce
45 grams	$1^1/_2$ ounces
55 grams	2 ounces
70 grams	$2^1/_2$ ounces
85 grams	3 ounces
100 grams	$3^1/_2$ ounces
110 grams	4 ounces
125 grams	$4^1/_2$ ounces
140 grams	5 ounces
280 grams	10 ounces
450 grams	16 ounces (1 pound)
500 grams	1 pound, $1^1/_2$ ounces
700 grams	$1^1/_2$ pounds
800 grams	$1^3/_4$ pounds
1 kilogram	2 pounds, 3 ounces
1.5 kilograms	3 pounds, $4^1/_2$ ounces
2 kilograms	4 pounds, 6 ounces

ABBREVIATION

tsp	teaspoon
Tbsp	tablespoon
g	gram
kg	kilogram
ml	millilitre

Heinz von Holzen

More than three decades ago, I planned a career in engineering. However, due to the lack of opportunities in the rural area of Switzerland where I grew up, I decided to take up an apprentice chef position instead. I figured that people would always have to eat and as such, chefs would always be in high demand. Following my apprenticeship I turned a childhood dream into reality when I started to travel and cook in European, Asian and Australian hotels. After $5^{1}/_{2}$ terrific years in Singapore where I was introduced to the many different flavours and cuisines of Asia, I received an opportunity to open the Grand Hyatt here on the Island of Gods.

Shortly after my arrival on this small Indonesian island, two of the best things in my life happened. I met my wife Puji and became involved with Balinese cuisine. Well, the arrival of our son Fabian would definitely rank before the discovery of Balinese cuisine. Eight years later, I made the decision to leave my position as Executive Chef at the prestigious Ritz Carlton Hotel in Bali in order to open my very own Balinese restaurant: Bumbu Bali, Restaurant & Cooking School. Never in my wildest dreams did I envision that I would get so much joy and success from this venture. What is more astonishing is that even after 15 years, Bumbu Bali, Restaurant & Cooking School remains the only restaurant in Bali to serve authentic Balinese cuisine in a beautiful traditional setting.

An important part of my daily ventures is the cooking classes which have given me an incredible amount of exposure around the globe. Conducted thrice weekly and limited to 14 participants, these classes provide a comprehensive insight into Balinese cuisine. The classes also inspire me to seek new trends and at the same time look a little deeper into the science of cooking which has become an integrated foundation of my daily activities.

Ida Bagus Wisnawa
Executive and Development Chef

Chef Bagus joined the opening team of the Grand Hyatt in Bali in 1991 as a trainee where he first met Heinz von Holzen, who was then the Executive Chef. Over the next 12 years, Pak Bagus worked hard and gradually climbed up the ranks of the kitchen hierarchy to the position of Chef de Cuisine where he was responsible for the operation of an entire kitchen. A 2-year assignment at Grand Hyatt, Dubai where he was in charge, preparing 2500 meals for breakfast, lunch and dinner, followed next.

After two years of hard work and because he was continuously home-sick, he returned to Bali and joined the team at Bumbu Bali, Restaurant & Cooking School in 2004. Over the past 9 years Pak Bagus has, with Heinz, travelled and cooked throughout Europe, the Middle East and also Indonesia in search of new dishes and recipes.

Pak Bagus has been the main person behind each and every dish that finds its way into the menu of Bumbu Bali or into one of the several books on which he has worked. Every new recipe created is carefully tested over and over again until its final stage, when the dish is served to regular customers. Pak Bagus' talent and never-ending passion for food have greatly contributed to this publication.